Music for Treviso Cathedral

ROYAL MUSICAL ASSOCIATION MONOGRAPHS

General editor: David Fallows

This series is supported by funds made available to the Royal Musical Association from the estate of Thurston Dart, former King Edward Professor of Music in the University of London. The editorial board is the Publications Committee of the Association.

No. 1: Playing on Words: a Guide to Luciano Berio's *Sinfonia* (1985) by David Osmond-Smith

No. 2: The Oratorio in Venice (1986) by Denis and Elsie Arnold

No. 3: Music for Treviso Cathedral in the Late Sixteenth Century: A Reconstruction of the Lost Manuscripts 29 and 30 (1987) by Bonnie J. Blackburn

ROYAL MUSICAL ASSOCIATION
MONOGRAPHS
3

Music for Treviso Cathedral in the Late Sixteenth Century

A Reconstruction of the Lost Manuscripts 29 and 30

BONNIE J. BLACKBURN

Royal Musical Association
London
1987

Published by the Royal Musical Association
Registered office c/o Waterhouse & Co., 4 St Paul's
Churchyard, London, EC4M 8BA

British Library Cataloguing in Publication Data

   Blackburn, Bonnie J.
     Music for Treviso Cathedral in the late
   sixteenth century: a reconstruction
   of the lost manuscripts 29 and 30. — (Royal
   Musical Association monographs; 3).
   1. Motet 2. Choral music — Italy —
   History and criticism
   I. Title II. Series
   783.4   ML2933

   ISBN 0 947854 02 9

Typeset by Alan Sutton Publishing Limited, Gloucester
Music examples by Tabitha Collingbourne, Newton Abbot

Printed in Great Britain
Design and production in association with
Alan Sutton Publishing Limited, Gloucester

Contents

Preface   vi

1 Introduction   1

2 The Repertory of MS 29 and its Liturgical Associations   4
The unica of MS 29   4
MS 29 and the liturgy of Treviso Cathedral   10
Table: The liturgical cycle   16

3 The Place of Motets in Liturgical Services   19
Motets arranged in liturgical cycles   19
The testimony of archival sources   21
The evidence of church choirbooks   29
The performance of motets in Treviso Cathedral   31

4 Sources and Physical Description of the Manuscripts   34
MS 29: sources   34
The repertory of MS 30   37
Physical description   43

5 The Newly Recovered Motets   46
Ghiselin Danckerts, *Tu es vas electionis a 5*   46
Ghiselin Danckerts, *Suscipe Verbum a 6*   51
Four motets by Trevisan choirmasters   52
Epilogue   55

Plates   56

Inventory   65
Sources   65
Abbreviations   69
Manuscript 29   72
Manuscript 30   106

Musical Appendix   114
1. Ghiselin Danckerts, *Suscipe Verbum Virgo Maria*   114
2. Pietro Antonio Spalenza, *Deus alma spes*   124
3. Francesco Santacroce, *Domine Deus omnipotens*   129
4. Giovanni Nasco, *Inviolata integra et casta es*   135
5. Giovanni Nasco, *Memor esto (1.p.)*   142

Index of Composers   145

Index of Compositions   149

General Index   154

Preface

The present study has had a long gestation. I discovered the clue to the puzzling repertory of the lost manuscript Treviso 29 while searching for concordances to the motets studied in my doctoral dissertation, 'The Lupus Problem' (University of Chicago, 1970). Over the years I have gradually fitted the pieces of the puzzle into place until a clear picture emerged. It may seem odd to speak of 'a clear picture' when dealing with a manuscript that has been destroyed and of which no microfilm exists. And yet, eight years ago, through the kindness of Father J. de Bruijn of Houten, Holland, I received photographs – unknown until now – of one composition from Treviso MS 29 and another from its companion volume, MS 30. This precious and quite unexpected gift has made it possible to recover a visual image of an unusual lost source and to relate it to the musical context in which it was created.

I owe thanks to a number of scholars who have helped me in various ways over the years. Professors H. Colin Slim and Charles Jacobs, on trips abroad, verified incipits. Professor Agostino Ziino sent photographs of a unique composition in the library of the Accademia di Santa Cecilia in Rome. Mgr Angelo Campagner, Director of the Biblioteca Capitolare, Treviso, graciously aided my search for pertinent material during a visit to Treviso in 1981. My husband, Edward E. Lowinsky, placed at my disposal the microfilms of material from the Biblioteca Capitolare that he made in Treviso in 1948, while Mgr Giovanni D'Alessi was still alive; without these, and without the research trips we took to Rome in 1977 and to Treviso in 1981, the present study could not have been written.

The method used in preparing this work owes much to the example set by James H. Moore in his investigation of Venetian music of the early seventeenth century. James Moore is sorely missed by all who knew him. For those who did not, the meticulous scholarship that characterizes his writings will remain a model for the approach to music through its relationship with liturgy and ceremonial. I should have liked to discuss many points in the present study with him; I regret that it was suddenly too late to do so. But he has aided me in another way, for I was able to use the microfilms he had collected for his studies of music at St Mark's, whose liturgy is closely linked to that of Treviso. It is with sadness and gratitude that I dedicate this monograph to his memory.

1
Introduction

Habent sua fata libelli. Who among us has not mourned the illuminated choirbook bereft of its initials, the forlorn fragments preserved in bindings, the palimpsest with its faint remains, the tantalizing descenders of a cropped name? The reconstruction of these mutilated manuscripts has demanded painstaking research and ingenuity. But what of the manuscripts that are completely lost – manuscripts we may know only from an entry in an account book or a listing in an inventory? The choirbook written by Josquin for the court of Milan seems beyond recovery; it was probably a casualty of the French invasion of Louis XII. Yet many manuscripts that belonged to the Sforza family, known from old inventories, have been identified in French libraries. Perhaps it too will be recovered one day. The Strasbourg MS 222 C. 22, burnt during the War of 1870, is not completely gone, for parts of it were copied by Coussemaker. Wars of all times have taken their toll of our musical heritage and especially the unique sources, musical manuscripts. With the advent of extensive microfilming, however, our musical patrimony stands a better chance of surviving wars and natural disasters.

More dismaying for music historians than the loss of a manuscript is the loss of whole repertories. For many court chapels, cathedrals and collegiate churches of the fifteenth and sixteenth centuries, famous for their polyphonic choirs, there is no trace of the choirbooks from which the singers sang. Especially grievous is the disappearance of the repertory of St Mark's under Willaert, Rore and Zarlino. In the face of such losses, the survival of the repertory of such important Italian centres as the Vatican, San Petronio in Bologna and Casale Monferrato has done much to expand our knowledge of sixteenth-century sacred music and its place in the liturgy.

One of the most extensive repertories of Renaissance sacred music that has come down to us was written for the Cathedral of Treviso, a small city seventeen miles north-west of Venice. The habit of the scribes of dating their work allows us to reconstruct the order of copying a large set of mid-sixteenth-century choirbooks containing Masses, hymns, motets, Magnificats, introits and alleluias, double-choir psalms and antiphons.[1] Eighteen of these choirbooks survived

---

[1] See the table and discussion in Charles Hamm, 'Interrelationships between Manuscript and Printed Sources of Polyphonic Music in the Early Sixteenth Century –

1

for four centuries, until 7 April 1944. On the 8th, only eleven remained, together with several other manuscripts of polyphonic music not forming part of the cathedral's original repertory.

On that fateful day of 7 April 1944, twenty-five manuscripts of polyphonic music written before 1630 and many prints in the cathedral's possession were destroyed, victims of an Allied raid over the city. The canons of the cathedral, during the early part of the war, had foreseen just such an eventuality, and they had charged Mgr Giovanni D'Alessi, then an assistant in the chapter library, with the difficult task of choosing the most precious documents for safe-keeping. The seventeen *casse* that were put at his disposal did not suffice for even a tenth of the material he felt needed preserving. By the time he had packed the oldest parchment documents, the incunabula, the rarest manuscripts, the papal bulls and the baptismal records prior to the Council of Trent, there was little room left for the music that D'Alessi had studied so lovingly.[2] Plans for the safe-keeping of further materials came to naught. In the last year of the war, the fears of the canons were realized. When the bombing began, D'Alessi relates, he was at home. As soon as the raid was over, he hastily made his way to the cathedral, where he found the library, though damaged on one side, still intact. But an incendiary bomb in the ruins of two houses near the church started a slow fire, which spread to the library. The telephones being out of order, a messenger was dispatched to the fire department outside the town. Delayed by other fires, the firemen arrived too late. Only the walls of the library resisted the conflagration.[3]

One week before the tragic event, D'Alessi had completed his book on the musical establishment of Treviso Cathedral from 1300 to 1633. He now had to include the sad news that only a small number of manuscripts and prints had survived.[4] His book, published ten years later, makes painfully clear the extent of that loss, for it contains, on pages 209 to 218, 'an alphabetical list of the authors with incipits of the texts of their compositions in manuscript existing in the Archivio Musicale on 7 April 1944'. D'Alessi did not provide a separate inventory of each manuscript, but from this list it is possible

---

An Overview', *Quellenstudien zur Musik der Renaissance II: Datierung und Filiation von Musikhandschriften der Josquin-Zeit*, ed. Ludwig Finscher (Wolfenbütteler Forschungen, 26; Wiesbaden, 1983), 1–13; pp. 5–6. A more extended discussion of this repertory may be found in the article on 'Sources, MS' in *The New Grove Dictionary of Music and Musicians*, 17 (London, 1980), under the section 'Renaissance polyphony, Italian cathedral and court manuscripts' by Charles Hamm and Jerry Call, pp. 692–3.

[2] See Giovanni D'Alessi, 'I manoscritti musicali del Sec. XVI° del Duomo di Treviso', *Acta musicologica*, 3 (1931), 148–55.

[3] D'Alessi's poignant description of these events is recorded in his book, *La Cappella musicale del Duomo di Treviso (1300–1633)* (Vedelago [Treviso], 1954), pp. 204–8.

[4] A list is given ibid., p. 208.

to reconstruct the contents (except for the anonymous pieces) of the lost manuscripts. That we know in detail what was destroyed makes that loss even more poignant.

2
The Repertory of MS 29 and its Liturgical Associations

The unica of MS 29

Among the lost manuscripts were two sets of part-books that did not belong to the cathedral's original repertory: MS 29, a set of five part-books, and MS 30, originally containing six part-books; the *Sexta pars* was missing before 1944.[1] I shall deal with the latter manuscript in Chapter 4. MS 29 belonged to Pietro Varisco, a priest whose entire career was spent at Treviso Cathedral, from his tonsure in 1550 to his death in 1584.[2] The part-books, bound in parchment, bore his coat of arms and initials: P(resbyter) P(etrus) V(ariscus).[3] Since they were part-books instead of the large choirbook normally used by church singers, they may have been copied by Varisco himself for his and his friends' use. If so, he must have been a musician and music lover of exceptional depth: MS 29 comprised no fewer than 175 motets, in two separate series, each of which had its own numbering.

From D'Alessi's alphabetical list of manuscript compositions in the chapter library, arranged by author, it is possible to draw up a list of the contents of MS 29. Varisco's part-books contained, as well as sixteen anonymous works, motets by the following composers (D'Alessi's spellings, some taken from different sources, are preserved):

Innocenzo Alberti: 1	Orlando di Lasso: 6
Giovanni Animuccia: 1	Giovanni Lupus: 1
Jakob Arcadelt: 1	Cristobal Morales: 2

---

[1] D'Alessi, *La Cappella musicale*, p. 185. See also the description in the *Census-Catalogue of Manuscript Sources of Polyphonic Music 1400–1550*, compiled by the University of Illinois Musicological Archives for Renaissance Manuscript Studies (Renaissance Manuscript Studies, Charles Hamm, general editor, 1; American Institute of Musicology and Hänssler Verlag, 1979–84), 3, pp. 248–9.

[2] See Giuseppe Liberali, *Lo stato personale del clero diocesano nel secolo XVI* (Documentari sulla Riforma Cattolica pre e post-Tridentina a Treviso, 1527–1577, 9; Treviso, 1975), p. 29, n. 44. He became a priest on 8 June 1555. His death is recorded in the chapter acts, which are no longer extant; see D'Alessi, *La Cappella musicale*, p. 179, n. 1.

[3] D'Alessi, *La Cappella musicale*, p. 179.

Arnoldi: 1
Bartolomeo Comes: 6
Giovanni Contino: 18
Gio. Battista Corvus: 3
Domenico Finot: 9
Gallicus: 1
Gislinus Danchera: 1
Bernardino Garilli: 3
Nicolas Gombert: 11
Jachet De Berchen: 3
Jachet: 9
Maistre Jan: 7
Lafage: 1

Giovanni Nasco: 2
Pierluigi Palestrina: 20
Francesco Patavino (Santacroce): 1
Pierreson: 1
Francesco Portinaro: 7
Jean Richafort: 1
Cipriano de Rore: 10
Enrico Scaffen: 1
Pierantonio Spalenza: 1
Guglielmo Testore: 1
Tugdual: 1
Adriano Willaert: 20
Gioseffo Zarlino: 8

Of these motets, the following do not appear under the name of the author in any other source and seem to be unica:[4]

Innocenzo Alberti
  Hic est dies egregius (no. 23)
Arcadelt
  Diem festum sacratissime (no. 8)
Jachet Berchem
  Gaude et laetare (second series, no. 34)
Bartholomeus Comes Gallicus
  Virgo martir (no. 14)
Jo. Continus
  Deus cuius dextera (no. 40)
  Intervenientibus Domine (no. 42)
  O quam magnificum (no. 49)
  Quia vidisti me Thoma (no. 78)
  Patefacte sunt ianue (no. 81)
  Benedictus qui venit (no. 85)
  Deus qui beatum (no. 94)
  Iste sanctus (no. 105)
  Sacerdos et pontifex (no. 112)
  Iste est qui ante Deum (no. 118)
Ghiselin Danckerts
  Tu es vas electionis (no. 9)
Domenico Finot
  Surge illuminare Jerusalem (no. 2)
  Descendit Spiritus Sanctus (no. 4)
  Agatha letissime (no. 13)
  Gabriel nunciavit Mariae (no. 19)
Nicolas Gombert
  Tu es Petrus (no. 15)
  Sancte Gregori (no. 16)
  In tua pacientia (no. 77)
  Juravit Dominus (no. 113)

---

[4] This list is based mainly on the motet catalogue of Edward Lowinsky, access to which eased my task considerably.

Jachet of Mantua
  O felix custos (no. 17)
  O praesul venerabilis (no. 67)
  Stans beata Agnes (no. 90)
  Similabo eum (no. 117)
Maitre Jhan
  Da ecclesie tue (no. 34)
  Sacre legis (no. 58)
  Ave Maria alta stirps (second series, no. 29)
Lafage
  Sancte Paule apostole (no. 39)
Lasso
  Antoni pater (no. 87)
  Elegit te Dominus (no. 93)
  O lux Italiae (no. 95)
  Qui vult venire (no. 106)
Lupi
  Sancte Marce evangelista (no. 20)
Jo. Nasco
  Inviolata (second series, no. 1)
Palestrina
  Beatus Dei famulus (no. 70)
  In medio ecclesiae (no. 82)
  Silvester beatissimus (no. 84)
  Filiae Jerusalem (no. 107)
  Haec est vera fraternitas (no. 111)
  Praeceptor bonum est (no. 131)
Perissonus (Cambio)
  Ave ignea columna (no. 75)
Portinaro
  Laudemus Deum (no. 91)
  Dum esset summus pontifex (no. 115)
Rore
  Mulier quae erat (no. 43)
  Hodie scietis (no. 79)
  Petre amas me (no. 88)
  O Gregori (no. 96)
  Laudemus Dominum (no. 98)
  Hic vir despiciens (no. 119)
  Prudentes virgines (no. 121)
  Regnum mundi (no. 123)
Scaffen
  Senex puerum portabat (no. 10)
Spalenza
  Deus alma spes (no. 71)
Testore
  In ferventis olei (no. 29)
Tugdual
  Gloriosum diem (no. 28)
Willaert
  O sodales sancti Vindemialis (no. 32)
  [O] Christi martir sancte Chiliane (no. 41)

Beatus Bernardus (no. 50)
Gaudeamus omnes (no. 59)
O doctor optime (no. 116)
Zarlino
Hodie sanctus Benedictus (no. 99)
Amavit eum Dominus (no. 114)

When we total the unica, the loss is enormous: no fewer than sixty-five works, among them motets by the most eminent composers of the time – Gombert, Lasso, Palestrina, Rore and Willaert – appear to be unique to Treviso 29. The same is true, to a lesser degree, of the other lost Treviso manuscripts. In his review of D'Alessi's book, Hans Albrecht remarked: 'Liest man dann das alphabetische Verzeichnis der Autoren der handschriftlich überlieferten Werke (mit den Text-Incipits der Kompositionen), dem ebenfalls der Stand vor dem 7. April 1944 zugrunde liegt, und kontrolliert mit Stichproben, was vernichtet ist, dann ist man erschüttert.'[5] Bernhard Meier, in his edition of Rore's *Opera omnia*, noted the loss of 'two central sources' (Treviso 29 and 30) that 'included nine motets by Rore, which have not been found in any other source'.[6] In the current literature – to take the articles in *The New Grove Dictionary* as an example – the lost works of MS 29 are mostly ignored,[7] and thus the presence of so many unica has not been noticed heretofore.

Giovanni D'Alessi, with extraordinary and perhaps unintended foresight, created an invaluable resource that was to become a memorial to the cathedral's lost manuscripts: a complete thematic index of every manuscript of polyphonic music before 1630. On specially prepared cards, he entered the number of the manuscript, the number of the composition, the author, the text incipit – often with indication of the liturgical occasion – the number of voices, and the first three or four notes in each part. Under *'Note'* he recorded canonic inscriptions and copyists' annotations (often dates). The cards were filed in the order within the manuscript and included anonymous compositions. Since they escaped destruction, they must have been kept in D'Alessi's home. Using these thematic incipits, now housed in the Biblioteca Capitolare, it has been possible to verify the textual incipits of MS 29 and to identify concordances under different names, with the result that several revisions can be made in the list given above: *Laudemus Dominum* (no. 98) was listed in D'Alessi's book under Rore by mistake; the card file attributes it to

---

[5] *Die Musikforschung*, 9 (1956), 250–4; p. 253.
[6] Bernhard Meier, ed., *Cipriani Rore Opera omnia*, 6 (Corpus mensurabilis musicae, 14; American Institute of Musicology, 1975), p. XIV.
[7] Exceptions are the articles on Danckerts (Lewis Lockwood, 5, p. 220), Gombert (George Nugent, 7, p. 515), Lupi (Blackburn, 11, p. 335), Rore (Alvin H. Johnson, 16, p. 188), Santacroce (Denis Arnold, 16, p. 475), Tugdual (Thomas W. Bridges, 19, p. 249), Willaert (Jessie Ann Owens, 20, pp. 426–7) and Zarlino (Claude V. Palisca, 20, p. 648).

Continus. *Gabriel nunciavit Mariae* (no. 19), ascribed in Treviso 29 to Phinot, occurs in other sources under the name of Gombert. *Ave Maria alta stirps* (second series, no. 29), attributed to 'Metre Jan', is identical with the motet on the same text by Jachet.[8] Phinot's *Surge illuminare Jerusalem* (no. 2) is the same as his *Illuminare Jerusalem*, found in a Gardane print of 1549.[9] Gombert's *Tu es Petrus* (no. 15) occurs under the name of Morales in two sources, and under Simon Moreau in a third. Maitre Jhan's *Da ecclesie tue* (no. 34) is preserved anonymously in Treviso 7, a source that has survived (three of his other motets, nos. 52, 55 and 58, had concordances in Treviso manuscripts now destroyed). A series of anonymous pieces (nos. 103, 124, and second series, nos. 9, 13, 23, 25, 27) can be identified with the same works (likewise anonymous) in Gardane's *Musica quinque vocum* (RISM 1549[6]). One of these works, *Virtute magna* (no. 103), is attributed to Rore in a print of 1595. Bernhard Meier included it in his edition of Rore's works, but he expressed doubts about its authenticity; he was unaware of the 1549 source, in which most of the motets are anonymous unica and none is attributed to Rore.[10]

These identifications notwithstanding, the number of unica has shrunk only slightly. It is puzzling why so many of the seemingly unique works come from the pen of major composers who had no connection with Treviso; in this case we cannot be dealing with a local repertory. But if we examine the texts, it would appear that a number of these pieces must have been composed specifically for Treviso Cathedral because they commemorate local saints: Liberalis, Florentius and Vindemialis, Hermacoras and Fortunatus, Prosdocimus, and Theonistus, Tabra and Tabrata.[11] It was Giovanni D'Alessi who uncovered the clue to this puzzle. But since it did not occur to him to wonder about the large number of unica – I do not know if he was aware of it – the clue has remained buried on page 215 of his book, within the list of works attributed to Palestrina. Under the entry of *Beatus Dei famulus – Gaude tarvisina civitas* (no. 70) he remarked:

---

[8] George Nugent, who was aware of the identity of the two pieces, states that 'on weighing the two [sources], the ascription to Jhan seems less trustworthy'; see 'The Jacquet Motets and their Authors' (Ph.D. dissertation, Princeton University, 1973), p. 201.

[9] The reading at Mass on Epiphany (Isaiah 60:1–6) begins *Surge, illuminare Jerusalem*, and this perhaps accounts for the addition of 'Surge' to the responsory text.

[10] See *Rore Opera omnia*, 6, p. XIII.

[11] Liberalis was the patron saint of Treviso. Hermacoras was a bishop of Aquileia; with his archdeacon Fortunatus, he was 'venerated in north-east Italy and specially at Padua, where he is the principal patron saint'; see S. J. P. Van Dijk, *Sources of the Modern Roman Liturgy*, 2 vols. (Studia et Documenta Franciscana, 1; Leiden, 1963), 1, p. 178. St Prosdocimus is a patron saint of Padua and was also venerated at St Mark's in Venice. The relics of SS Florentius and Vindemialis lie in Treviso Cathedral, as do those of SS Theonistus, Tabra and Tabrata. The only saint who seems to have no connection with Treviso is St Kylianus (8 July). Born in Ireland or Scotland in the seventh century, he became the patron saint of Würzburg (*Acta Sanctorum*, 8 July).

'adattamento del testo sul mottetto "Gaude Barbara". Cfr. Mottetti a 5, 6, e 8 voci Libro II – Venezia 1577' – a print formerly in the possession of the chapter.[12] It was not Palestrina, then, who set to music this text for the feast of SS Theonistus, Tabra and Tabrata, whose bodies rest in Treviso Cathedral, but someone else, most probably Pietro Varisco himself, who took Palestrina's motet and adapted it to the text of an antiphon at Lauds for this feast day, 22 November.[13]

Facile est inventis addere: once the clue was discovered, solving the puzzle of MS 29's numerous unica proved easy. The five other unique pieces attributed to Palestrina (nos. 82, 84, 107, 111 and 131) are taken from Palestrina's Book II and Book III of motets for five, six and eight voices, with altered texts. Altogether I have identified sixty contrafacta (see the Inventory below for details) of works by the following composers, including all of the remaining *anonymi*:[14]

1	Arcadelt (no. 8)
2	Comes (nos. 14 and 53)
15	Contino (nos. 40, 42, 49, 51, 54, 60, 66, 78, 81, 85, 94, 98, 105, 112, 118)
2	Gombert (nos. 77 and 113)
4	Jachet (nos. 17, 67, 90, 117)
1	Lafage (no. 39)
4	Lasso (nos. 87, 93, 95, 106)
2	Lupi (nos. 16 and 20)
6	Palestrina (nos. 70, 82, 84, 107, 111, 131)
1	Perissone (Cambio) (no. 75)
3	Phinot (nos. 4, 9, 13)
2	Portinaro (nos. 91 and 115)
7	Rore (nos. 43, 79, 88, 96, 119, 121, 123)
1	Testore (no. 29)
1	Verdelot (no. 22)
6	Willaert (nos. 32, 41, 50, 57, 59, 116)
2	Zarlino (nos. 99, 114)

The number of unica now stands at five (nos. 10, 23, 71, II/1, II/34). With the exception of nos. 41 and 57, all contrafacta were made from motets. The choice of works reflects astonishingly well the reputation of the various composers both then and today (taking into account their generations), with the one exception of Contino.

---

[12] D'Alessi, *La Cappella musicale*, p. 198.

[13] As specified in the 1524 Ordinal of Treviso Cathedral, about which below.

[14] The incipits, taken from D'Alessi's card catalogue, are given in the Inventory below. Since they are very short – two or three notes in each part – some of the identifications may not be certain. It is possible for two motets to have exactly the same opening but then diverge. A case in point from a different repertory: the first five and a half bars of Crecquillon's *Sancta Maria Virgo virginum* are identical with the same bars of Clemens non Papa's *Ascendit Deus in jubilatione*, and the four lower voices are identical until bar 8; see Edward Lowinsky, 'Zur Frage der Deklamationsrhythmik in der a-cappella-Musik des 16. Jahrhunderts', *Acta musicologica*, 7 (1935), 62–7.

Manuscript 29 and the liturgy of Treviso Cathedral

Why did Varisco, if he is the person responsible, undertake to manufacture so many 'new' compositions? The answer lies in the texts. Like most of the motet manuscripts that belonged to the cathedral, MS 29 was arranged in liturgical order.[15] Two series can be discerned: nos. 1–79 run from Christmas to Christmas eve (see the Inventory below). No. 80 begins a new liturgical cycle with Christmas, partly duplicating feasts in the first cycle, but ending with the Feast of St Benedict on 21 March (no. 99). Then follow motets appropriate to the Common of Saints: Apostles and Evangelists (no. 100), Apostles (nos. 101–2), Apostles in Paschaltide (no. 103), One Martyr (nos. 104–6), Apostles and Martyrs in Paschaltide (no. 107), Martyrs (nos. 108–10), Two or More Martyrs (no. 111), a Confessor Bishop (nos. 112–15), Doctors (no. 116), a Confessor not a Bishop (nos. 117–19), Virgins (nos. 120, 124), Two or More Virgin Martyrs (no. 121), Virgins and Holy Women (no. 122), Holy Women (no. 123), and Dedication of a Church (nos. 125–7). At the end of the first section comes a supplement of five motets, also in liturgical order (nos. 128–32). The motets are for fixed feasts and destined mostly for the Sanctoral Cycle; the only part of the Temporal Cycle represented is feasts from Christmas to Epiphany.

Since the manuscript no longer exists, we cannot tell why there were two separate liturgical cycles. The second is much more complete for the period 26 December to 1 January, filling a gap in the first sequence. Perhaps Varisco added these motets at a later time.[16] The second part of the manuscript, which had its own numbering (second series, nos. 1–43), consisted exclusively of Marian motets, most of a general nature, but some appropriate to certain feasts: Annunciation (nos. 4, 27, 37), Visitation (nos. 18, 24), Assumption (nos. 5, 16), Nativity of the Virgin (no. 15), Christmas (nos. 33, 40), Immaculate Conception (nos. 8, 42) and Purification (no. 43).

The liturgy of Treviso Cathedral differed from the Roman rite in the number of feasts and their degree of solemnity. Like the liturgy of St Mark's in Venice, it preserved elements of the Aquileian rite, which was widely used in northern Italy before the reforms set in motion by the Council of Trent.[17] In his papal bull of 1568, *Quod a nobis*, Pius V mandated the uniform adoption of the newly revised

---

[15] On the liturgical ordering of the repertories of MSS 4, 5, 6, 7 and 8, the dates of copying, and the polyphonic repertory of the cathedral in general, see the excellent description by Charles Hamm and Jerry Call in *The New Grove Dictionary* (see above, Chapter 1, n. 1). MSS 29, 30 and 36 are not included, perhaps because they are not choirbooks and did not form part of the repertory that was copied for the cathedral choir.

[16] According to D'Alessi's card catalogue, no dates were entered into the part-books.

[17] James H. Moore has sketched the relations between Venice and Aquileia from the time Venice stole the relics of St Mark from Alexandria ca. 828–9 – thus usurping Aquileia's patron saint – until 1807, when the patriarchate of Aquileia was transferred

breviary of 1568, but he made an exception for churches that could prove that their liturgies went back further than two hundred years. The liturgy of St Mark's fell into this category, and the Procurators, as James Moore notes, exploited this 'escape clause' fully.[18] It should be recalled that St Mark's was the ducal chapel and as such was the focus of civic as well as religious ceremonies, so much so that 'the resplendent ceremonial life of St Mark's was considered a symbol of the state'.[19] The Duomo of Treviso did not hold the same position in the government of the city, but the ecclesiastical hierarchy felt no less pride in its special liturgy, as is evident from the preface of Clemens a Stadiis to the Ordinal he revised and copied for the cathedral in 1524:

God is glorified by the offering of praise, and that is the road to salvation which, it is clear, is to be taken by all, each in his own way. The holy universal church uses the Gregorian rite; the patriarchal churches, however, and those subject to them follow partly the same rite and partly a different one: whence it comes that our Trevisan church makes use of a rite differing in many ways, one most praiseworthy and approved and transmitted from hand to hand rather than otherwise[20] by our forefathers and happily observed down to our own day.[21]

---

to St Mark's; see *Vespers at St. Mark's: Music of Alessandro Grandi, Giovanni Rovetta and Francesco Cavalli*, 2 vols. (Studies in Musicology, 30; Ann Arbor, 1981), 1, pp. 122–3 (all subsequent references are to volume 1). Scholars have long argued over the origin of St Mark's special liturgy; by a careful comparison of Aquileian breviaries, the *Orationale* of St Mark's and the Roman rite, Moore has been able to show that 'the textual content of the liturgy in St. Mark's differs from Rome in countless details, many of which can be traced to Aquileian sources' (ibid., p. 122).

[18] Ibid., p. 112.

[19] Ibid., p. 153. In her article on 'Music in the Myth of Venice' (*Renaissance Quarterly*, 30 [1977], 511–37), Ellen Rosand gives a panorama of 'the crescendo of musical activity in Cinquecento Venice', which was, as she documents, 'carefully planned, encouraged, and carried out by the state, . . . accompanied by constant affirmation on the part of the *Procuratori* and by the Doge himself of the importance of official music to the image of Venice. Nearly every appointment document, no matter how apparently minor, carries with it a weighty declaration about its significance to the state' (p. 524).

[20] Perhaps 'per manus . . . tradito' should be translated as 'transmitted in writing', since the author seems to imply that the manuscript tradition is more trustworthy than oral transmission (*potius quam aliter*).

[21] 'Sacrificio laudis glorificatur Deus: et illud est iter ad salutem quod multipliciter fieri ab omnibus liquet: sancta etenim universalis ecclesia Gregoriano officio utitur: Patriarchales vero ecclesiae et illis subiectae partim eodem modo, et etiam partim diverso: Inde est quod ecclesia nostra Tarvisina alieno in pluribus ordine utitur plurimum laudabili et approbato, ac per manus potius, quam aliter a maioribus tradito: Et usque ad nostra tempora foeliciter observato . . .'; *Ordinarium divini officii iuxta consuetudinem Cathedralis Ecclesiae Tarvisinae per totum anni circulum celebrandi cotidie*. The 150-page manuscript, housed in the Biblioteca Capitolare of the Duomo, is written on paper in one hand, with some notes added by other hands. On the verso of the title page the scribe has signed and dedicated his work: 'Clemens a Stadijs ecclesiae Cathedralis Tarvisinae Mansionarius: Venerandis sacerdotibus et orthodoxae fidei cultoribus salutem in Domino'. The date of copying appears on fol.1: 'Anno Salutiferi Natalis eiusdem D(omini) n(ostri) yhesu christi. M.D.xxiiij'. ('Mansionarius' denotes a member of the plainchant choir.)

Clemens a Stadiis was 'maestro di canto fermo' at the cathedral in 1528.[22] His Ordinal allows us to reconstruct the liturgy used at Treviso Cathedral and to determine the liturgical placement of the motets in MS 29. The Table (pp. 16–18) lists the duplex feasts (those with the most solemn celebration, 'duplex' referring to two Vesper services) observed at the cathedral and all other feasts for which motets were provided. For comparison, other columns show the position of these feasts in the liturgy of St Mark's, the liturgy of Aquileia and the Roman rite, after a pre-Tridentine *Breviarium* of 1562.

The Trevisan Ordinal has three ranks of feasts: duplex, semiduplex and simplex (the last is not so labelled, but is to be assumed when no other rank is listed). In every case but sixteen, a fixed feast marked as duplex in the calendar of the Ordinal has at least one motet in MS 29. Eleven of the exceptions are the following: the Octave commemorations of St Stephen (2 January), St John (3 January) and Holy Innocents (4 January), the Translation of St Mark (31 January), the Commemoration of St Paul (30 June), the Chains of St Peter (1 August), the Exaltation of the Holy Cross (13 September), the Dedication of St Michael (29 September), the Dedication of the Church of St Mark (8 October), the Dedication of the Basilica of the Saviour (9 November) and the Dedication of the Basilicas of SS Peter and Paul (18 November). But for all of these, motets for other feasts honouring the same saints could have been used, and the three motets for the Common of the Dedication of a Church (nos. 125–7) could have served the three specific Dedications.[23]

Only five duplex feasts in the Sanctoral Cycle at Treviso Cathedral lack an appropriate motet in MS 29: St Titianus (19 January), the Forty Holy Martyrs (9 March), St Longinus (14 March), St Patrick (17 March) and St Barnabas (11 June). For any of these feasts, however, one of the motets for the Common of Saints (nos. 100–19) could have been sung. It is also possible that the calendar changed between 1524 and 1584, the *terminus ante quem* for the copying of MS 29, and that some of these feasts were reduced in rank. That feasts were newly created after 1524 is shown by the presence of three motets in MS 29 for feasts not listed in the Ordinal: 18 January appears in the Ordinal as the feast of St Prisca, Virgin and Martyr, of semiduplex rank; MS 29

---

[22] D'Alessi, *La Cappella musicale*, p. 70.

[23] In January of 1595 Francesco Veretoni, a singer at the cathedral, prepared an inventory of the musical manuscripts (which does not include MS 29, probably because it was not a choirbook) together with an index of feasts beginning with 1 May (SS Philip and James) and ending with 27 April (St Liberalis), with references to the volume and page numbers of motets appropriate to each feast. The inventory also contained an alphabetical list of the motets with reference to the volume containing them (ibid., p. 180; Veretoni's catalogue of manuscripts is transcribed on pp. 181–2). Unfortunately, the inventory did not escape destruction, so we have no way of telling whether the motets of MS 29 were entered into the index of feasts, even if the manuscript itself does not appear on the list. This system of cross-references would have facilitated the choice of motets for feasts.

has instead a motet for the feast of the Chair of St Peter at Rome. This feast was instituted by Paul IV in 1558.[24] The Ordinal gives 16 August to the feast of St Leonard; MS 29 has instead a motet for the feast of St Roch. In this case, however, a later hand has added the feast of St Roch on fol. 127v, with the note 'omnia sicut in festo duplici'. The feast of St Joachim on 20 March, for which one motet is provided, does not appear in the Ordinal.

A comparison with the liturgies of St Mark's, Aquileia and the Roman rite shows that Treviso Cathedral celebrated a much larger number of feasts at the highest rank. St Mark's divided feasts into four categories: duplex maius, duplex minus, semiduplex and simple. Nearly all feasts that St Mark's celebrated as semiduplex or even simple Treviso treated as duplex. The discrepancies are even greater with the liturgy of Aquileia, which has five ranks of feasts, reminiscent of the monastic rite: duplex maius, duplex (minus), cum pleno officio, novem lectiones and tres lectiones (nine or three lessons at Matins). Similarly, the Trevisan rite has many more duplex feasts than the Roman rite. That this meant more work for the choirmasters is shown in a letter Giovanni Nasco wrote to the Accademia Filarmonica on 10 January 1553, apologizing for not sending more new compositions because 'le feste mi hanno molto impedito'.[25] In the preceding sixteen days, he had directed the choir on nine duplex feasts; in the Roman rite he would have been responsible for only five.

The greater degree of liturgical solemnity at Treviso and the presence of a number of local saints not found in the Roman breviary placed special demands on the compiler of MS 29 if he wished to include an outstanding work of polyphonic music in five or six voices for each duplex feast. His solution was to provide contrafactum texts; the motets for most of the feasts just named are contrafacta, with the notable exception of Pietro Antonio Spalenza's *Deus alma spes* (no. 71) for the feast of SS Theonistus, Tabra and Tabrata. Spalenza, a native of Brescia, became director of the choir at Treviso at the latest by 24

---

[24] See Ludwig Eisenhofer and Joseph Lechner, *The Liturgy of the Roman Rite*, trans. A. J. and E. F. Peeler, ed. H. E. Winstone (Freiburg and Edinburgh–London, 1961), p. 236. The new feast is not yet present in the breviary of 1562 used in the Table.

A number of changes were incorporated in the reformed breviary issued by Pius V in 1568. Feasts were restricted to three classes: duplex, semiduplex, and simplex. The following feasts listed in the Table were raised to duplex: 28 and 31 December, 2, 3, 4, 13, 17, 20 and 21 January, 10 March (but celebrated on 7 March, as in Aquileia and at St Mark's), 8 May, 22 July, 4, 20 and 29 August, 11 and 25 November, and 13 December. The following feasts were dropped from universal observance: Translation of St Mark (31 January), St Longinus (14 March), St Patrick (17 March), St Anthony of Padua (13 June), Octave of the Visitation (9 July), SS Hermacoras and Fortunatus (22 July), St Anne (26 July), St Roch (16 August), St Prosdocimus (7 November), and Presentation of the Virgin (21 November); some of these feasts may also have been omitted in the liturgy of Treviso after 1568, since MS 29 has no motets for 31 January, 14 and 17 March, 9 July and 21 November.

[25] D'Alessi, *La Cappella musicale*, p. 108.

April 1573; he was no longer alive on 27 May 1577.[26] The presence of Spalenza's motet in the first liturgical cycle of MS 29 makes it likely that the copying of the manuscript did not begin before the 1570s. (The evidence of the concordances, discussed below, confirms this dating.)

Other contrafacta were made for feasts common to the Trevisan and Roman rites, but to texts that one will not easily find in the repertory of the sixteenth-century motet; for example: *Diem festum sacratissime* (no. 8; responsory for the Feast of St Agnes, 21 January),[27] *Agatha laetissime* (no. 13; responsory for the Feast of St Agatha, 5 February), *O felix custos* (no. 17; antiphon for the Feast of St Joseph, 19 March), *In ferventis olei* (no. 29; antiphon for the Feast of St John before the Lateran Gate, 6 May), *Mulier quae erat* (no. 43; antiphon for the Feast of St Mary Magdalene, 22 July), *Beatus Bernardus* (no. 50; antiphon for the Feast of St Bernard of Clairvaux, 20 August), *Misit rex incredulus* (no. 53; two antiphons for the Feast of the Beheading of St John the Baptist, 29 August), *Ave ignea columna* (no. 75; St Ambrose, 7 December), *Silvester beatissimus* (no. 84; antiphon for the Feast of St Silvester, 31 December), *Hodie sanctus Benedictus* (no. 99; antiphon for the Feast of St Benedict, 21 March). On the other hand, contrafacta also appear to texts that belong to the Common of Saints and are not unusual. Here Varisco must have made a musical decision, choosing works of his particular liking by Contino (nos. 105, 112, 118), Lasso (no. 106), Palestrina (nos. 107, 111), Gombert (no. 113), Zarlino (no. 114), Portinaro (no. 115), Willaert (no. 116), Jachet (no. 117) and Rore (nos. 119, 121, 123). The contrafacta are entirely confined to the first series; of Marian motets there was no dearth of settings. The practice of substituting texts seems unique to MS 29 (with one exception; see the Inventory, no. 39) and does not represent a tradition at the cathedral.

Whereas the motets of MS 29 are arranged in the liturgical cycle of the cathedral, the texts often do not coincide with antiphons or responsories specified for those feasts in the Ordinal of Clemens a Stadiis. For example, at Second Vespers on the Feast of SS Fabian and Sebastian (20 January), Clemens lists the antiphons *Sebastianus Dei cultor* and *Egregie Dei martir*. For the first, Zarlino's motet (no. 89) is appropriate; for the second, MS 29 provides instead Gombert's responsory setting, *Egregie martir Sebastiane* (when Moderne published this motet, he omitted the name of the saint). For the Feast of St Blaise (3 February), the Ordinal carries the statement 'Totum

---

[26] Ibid., pp. 123–4. Seven of his works once existed in the cathedral library (ibid., p. 125). It is perhaps through the initiative of Spalenza that Contino's works became known to Varisco; Contino was *maestro di cappella* at Brescia Cathedral from 1551 to 1566 (*The New Grove Dictionary*, 4, p. 684), and Spalenza, a native of Brescia, may very well have been a choirboy there during his tenure. Nothing is known of his career before 1573, but he seems to have died young, since his heirs petitioned the chapter for assistance after his death. Pier Paolo Scattolin gives a birth date of ca. 1545 in *The New Grove Dictionary*, 17, p. 814.

[27] On the liturgical sources of these texts, see the Inventory below.

officium fit de communi unius martiris' (fol. 102), listing no specific chants. Manuscript 29 has two motets for St Blaise. Two antiphons are assigned to Vespers on the Feast of St Mary Magdalene (22 July), neither of which is *Mulier quae erat*, the contrafactum text of Rore's *Domine quis habitabit*. Similarly, the Ordinal lists neither of the texts in MS 29 for the Feast of St Prosdocimus (nos. 66–7).

The majority of the texts set are antiphons and responsories, and in a liturgically oriented manuscript, this is not surprising. Of the 175 texts (only six of which are duplicated), I have been unable to identify thirty-three. Since the incipits given by D'Alessi are rather short and the texts of many of the motets are no longer extant, a note of caution about the possibility of 'identifying' the texts is in order. Bearing this in mind, the results are as follows:

> antiphons: 70[28]
> responsories: 40[29]
> prayers: 8
> Bible verses: 5
> sequences: 4
> hymns: 3
> rhymed poems: 2
> invitatories: 2
> Gospel settings: 2
> communions: 2
> Gospel and antiphon: 1
> introit and verse of Gradual: 1
> Graduals: 1
> short responsories: 1

The evidence shows that although MS 29 is organized in two liturgical cycles, the music itself cannot be considered liturgical. Many of the texts have no place in the Trevisan liturgy. Moreover, when a liturgical text is used, it can be handled fairly freely. Consider the responsory motets made up of the first part of two different responsories and the antiphon motets combining two or three different antiphons. It is clear that these motets were not meant to replace the Gregorian chants. Nor do their texts fit a single occasion, such as Vespers or Mass, where polyphonic settings are most frequently used. The motets of MS 29 were chosen because they are appropriate to the feast. Even the contrafactum texts, a number of which have not been identified, are only partially found in the Trevisan liturgy.[30] We shall have to look elsewhere to answer the question when these motets were performed.

---

[28] Three motet texts are made up of two antiphons (nos. 53, 77 and II/10), one of three antiphons (no. 63).

[29] Five motets appear to be based on the first part of the responsory only (nos. 26, 36, 85, II/5, II/27), and three motets are made up of two responsory texts without the versus (nos. 2, 8, 28).

[30] In the Inventory below, those texts whose source is listed as *Ordinarium* have been found only in the liturgy of Treviso.

Liturgical cycle of MS Treviso 29 compared with the liturgies of Treviso, St Mark's, Aquileia and the Roman rite

Date	Feast	Motets in Treviso 29	Treviso[a]	St Mark's[b]	Aquileia[c]	Roman rite[d]
December						
25	Christmas	1, 80, II/33, 40	duplex	maius duplex	duplex maius	duplex maius
26	St Stephen	81	duplex	duplex maius	duplex	duplex maius
27	St John Apostle	82	duplex	duplex maius	duplex	duplex maius
28	Holy Innocents	83	duplex	duplex minus	duplex	semiduplex
31	St Silvester	84	[simplex]	duplex minus	9 lectiones	semiduplex
January						
1	Circumcision	85	duplex	duplex maius	maius duplex	duplex minus
2	Octave of St Stephen		duplex	semiduplex	9 lectiones	semiduplex
3	Octave of St John		duplex ·	semiduplex	9 lectiones ·	semiduplex
4	Octave of Holy Innocents		duplex	semiduplex	9 lectiones	semiduplex
6	Epiphany	2, 3, 86	duplex	duplex maius	maius duplex	duplex maius
13	Octave of Epiphany	4	duplex	semiduplex	9 lectiones	semiduplex
17	St Anthony Abbot	5, 6, 87	semiduplex	duplex minus	9 lectiones	solemne generaliter
18	Chair of St Peter at Rome[e]	88	St Prisca semiduplex	duplex minus[f]	—	St Prisca [simplex]
19	St Titianus		duplex	—	—	—
20	SS Fabian and Sebastian	7, 89	duplex	duplex minus	9 lectiones	[simplex]
21	St Agnes	8, 90	semiduplex	semiduplex	9 lectiones	semiduplex
25	Conversion of St Paul	9, 91	duplex	duplex minus	duplex	duplex minus
31	Translation of St Mark		duplex	duplex maius	9 lectiones	duplex minus
February						
2	Purification	10, 11, II/43	duplex	duplex maius	maius duplex	duplex maius
3	St Blaise	12, 92	duplex	[simplex]	9 lectiones	[simplex]
5	St Agatha	13	semiduplex	semiduplex	9 lectiones	semiduplex
9	St Apollonia	14	semiduplex	[simplex]	[simplex][g]	[simplex]
22	Chair of St Peter at Antioch	15, 93	duplex	duplex minus	cum pleno officio	duplex minus
24	St Matthias	94	duplex	duplex minus	duplex	duplex maius
March						
9	Forty Martyrs		duplex	[simplex]	9 lectiones (on 11 March)	[simplex]
10	St Thomas Aquinas	95	duplex	[simplex] (on 7 March)	9 lectiones (on 7 March)	—
12	St Gregory	16, 96	duplex	duplex minus	duplex	duplex minus
14	St Longinus		duplex	[simplex] (on 15 March)	—	[simplex] (on 15 March)
17	St Patrick		duplex	[simplex]	—	[simplex]
19	St Joseph	17, 97	duplex	duplex minus	[simplex][g]	duplex maius
20	St Joachim	98	—	[simplex]	—	—
21	St Benedict	99	semiduplex	duplex minus	cum pleno officio	duplex minus
25	Annunciation	18, 19, II/4, 27, 37	duplex	duplex maius	maius duplex	duplex maius
April						
25	St Mark	20, 21	duplex	duplex maius	duplex	duplex minus
27	St Liberalis	22, 23	duplex	[simplex]	—	—
May						
1	SS Philip and James	24, 25	duplex	duplex minus	duplex	duplex minus
3	Finding of Holy Cross	26–8	semiduplex	duplex minus	cum pleno officio	duplex minus

Date	Feast	Motets in Treviso 29	Treviso[a]	St Mark's[b]	Aquileia[c]	Roman rite[d]
6	St John before Lateran Gate	29	duplex	duplex minus	9 lectiones	duplex minus
8	Victory of St Michael	30	semiduplex	duplex minus	9 lectiones	semiduplex
June						
1	SS Florentius and Vindemialis	31, 32	duplex	—	—	—
11	St Barnabas		duplex	duplex minus	duplex	duplex minus
13	St Anthony of Padua	33	semiduplex	duplex minus	9 lectiones	duplex maius
15	SS Vitus and Modestus	34	duplex	duplex minus	9 lectiones	[simplex]
24	Nativity of St John Baptist	35, 36, 129	duplex	duplex maius	duplex	duplex maius
29	SS Peter and Paul	37–9	duplex	duplex maius	duplex	duplex maius
30	Commemoration of St Paul		duplex	duplex minus	duplex	duplex
July						
2	Visitation	II/18, 24	duplex	duplex maius	duplex	duplex maius
6	Octave of SS Peter and Paul	40	duplex	duplex minus	3 lectiones	duplex minus
8	St Kylianus and Companions	41	duplex	—	—	—
9	Octave of Visitation		duplex	duplex minus	—	duplex minus
12	SS Hermacoras and Fortunatus	42	duplex	duplex minus	duplex maius	[simplex]
22	St Mary Magdalene	43	duplex	duplex minus	cum pleno officio	semiduplex
25	St James	44, 130	duplex	duplex minus	duplex	duplex minus
26	St Anne	45	duplex	duplex minus	[simplex][g]	duplex maius
August						
1	Chains of St Peter		duplex	duplex minus	cum pleno officio	duplex minus
4	St Dominic	46	[duplex]	duplex minus	—	—
6	Transfiguration	47, 131	duplex	duplex maius	[simplex][g]	duplex maius
10	St Lawrence	48	duplex	duplex minus	duplex	duplex maius
15	Assumption	II/5, 16	duplex	duplex maius	maius duplex	duplex maius
16	St Roch[h]	49	duplex	[simplex]	—	[simplex]
20	St Bernard of Clairvaux	50	[simplex]	[simplex]	9 lectiones	[simplex]
24	St Bartholomew	51, 132	duplex	duplex minus	duplex	duplex minus
28	St Augustine	52	duplex	duplex minus	duplex	duplex minus
29	Beheading of St John Baptist	53	[duplex]	duplex minus	cum pleno officio[i]	semiduplex
September						
8	Nativity of B.V.M.	II/15	duplex	duplex maius	maius duplex	duplex maius
14	Exaltation of Holy Cross		duplex	duplex minus	cum pleno officio	duplex minus
21	St Matthew	54	duplex	duplex minus	duplex	duplex minus
29'	Dedication of St Michael		duplex	duplex minus	duplex	duplex minus
30	St Jerome	55	duplex	[simplex]	duplex	duplex minus
October						
4	St Francis	56	duplex	duplex minus	9 lectiones	duplex minus
7	St Justina	57	duplex	[simplex][j]	St Mark, Pope, duplex	—
8	Dedication of Church of St Mark		duplex	duplex maius	—	—
18	St Luke	58	duplex	duplex minus	duplex	duplex minus
21	11,000 Virgins	59	duplex	[simplex]	9 lectiones	[simplex]
28	SS Simon and Jude	60	duplex	duplex minus	duplex	duplex minus

17

Date	Feast	Motets in Treviso 29	Treviso[a]	St Mark's[b]	Aquileia[c]	Roman rite[d]
November						
1	All Saints	61–5	duplex	duplex maius	maius duplex	duplex maius
7	St Prosdocimus	66, 67	duplex	[simplex]	—	[simplex]
9	Dedication of Basilica of the Saviour		duplex	St Theodore duplex minus	St Theodore 9 lectiones	duplex maius
11	St Martin	68, 69	duplex	duplex minus	cum pleno officio	semiduplex
18	Dedication of Basilicas of SS Peter and Paul		duplex	duplex minus	Octave of St Martin 3 lectiones	duplex maius
21	Presentation of B.V.M.		duplex	duplex maius	St Maurus 3 lectiones	duplex maius
22	SS Theonistus, Tabra, Tabrata	70, 71	semiduplex[k]	[simplex][l]	St Cecilia 9 lectiones	—
25	St Catherine	72, 128	duplex	duplex minus	cum pleno officio	semiduplex et solemne generaliter
30	St Andrew	73	duplex	duplex minus	duplex	duplex minus
December						
6	St Nicholas	74	duplex	duplex minus	cum pleno officio	semiduplex et solemne generaliter
7	St Ambrose	75	duplex	duplex minus	duplex	duplex minus
8	Conception of B.V.M.	II/8, 42	duplex	duplex maius	duplex	duplex maius
13	St Lucy	76, 77	duplex	duplex minus	cum pleno officio	semiduplex et solemne generaliter
21	St Thomas Apostle	78	duplex	duplex minus	duplex	duplex minus
24	Vigil of Christmas	79	duplex	Vigilia	duplex	Vigilia

[a] *Ordinarium divini officii iuxta consuetudinem Cathedralis Ecclesiae Tarvisinae*, MS copied in 1524 (Treviso, Biblioteca Capitolare).

[b] *Orationale ad usum Basilicae Ducalis Sancti Marci Venetiarum* (Venice, Biblioteca del Civico Museo Correr, Codice Cicogna 1602), copied in 1567 (Moore, *Vespers at St. Mark's*, 1, p. 114). The calendar for January, missing in the manuscript, is supplied from the *Caeremoniale rituum sacrorum ecclesiae S. Marci Venetiarum* of Bartolomeo Bonifacio, dated 1564 (Venice, Biblioteca Nazionale Marciana, Cod. Lat. III–172 [=2276], fol. 33v) (Moore, *Vespers*, 1, p. 69).

[c] *Breviarium secundum ritum et consuetudinem alme ecclesie Aquileiensis* (Venice: Franciscus de Hailbrun, 1481) and, for feasts added after 1481, *Modus et ordo cerimonialium et quorundam actuum ecclesiasticorum totius anni ad usum Sancte Ecclesie Aquilegiensis* (Venice: Aegidius Regazola, 1575).

[d] *Breviarium Romanum optime recognitum: in quo Commune sanctorum cum suis psalmis, Nonnulle Octave, Tabula parisina, Officium nominis Jesu, Desponsationis Marie et alia multa, que in ceteris desiderabantur, nuper sunt accommodata* (Venice: Jo. Variscus, 1562). On changes made in the 1568 breviary, see Chapter 2, n. 24 above.

[e] This feast was introduced in 1558.

[f] Added in a later hand.

[g] Feast in 1575 only.

[h] The regular feast in the *Ordinarium* is St Leonard; St Roch was added in a different hand at a later place.

[i] Duplex in 1575.

[j] The main feast is SS Sergius and Bacchus, duplex minus.

[k] The main feast is St Cecilia; St Theonistus and Companions is listed as semiduplex.

[l] The main feast is St Cecilia, semiduplex.

3
The Place of Motets in Liturgical Services

One of the many problems facing historians of early music concerns the function of motets. The size of the repertory is enormous, but information about its function is scarce. Are we right in assuming that the text is a clear indicator of liturgical use? This is a question that occupies musical scholars today far more than it did musicians of the time. Theorists do not discuss the subject. Certainly it is obvious that the vast majority of the repertory is sacred music, destined for church services. The motets of Treviso 29 were organized according to the liturgical calendar. But it is hard to ascertain where they were sung in services, since their texts are so disparate and, in many cases, so tenuously linked with the liturgy of Treviso. To answer this question we must turn to contemporary sources that have a bearing on the problem: repertories of music in which the liturgical placement is indicated for each piece, and records of religious establishments that mention the singing of motets. Some of the evidence adduced below comes from the early years of the seventeenth century. I believe, however, that it is valid for late sixteenth-century sources such as Treviso 29. The year 1600 is an artificial dividing line between Renaissance and Baroque music and may be pushed in one direction or the other, depending on what genres or styles we speak about. Little change is discernible in the function of motets, especially within institutions; as will be seen in documents cited below, motets of the 1550s are still being sung in the second decade of the seventeenth century and in the same places in the services.

Motets arranged in liturgical cycles

The evidence connecting individual motets with specific liturgical occasions is sparse in sixteenth-century sources; if they are arranged in a liturgical cycle, usually no more information is given than the name of the appropriate feast, and even this is not common. The early seventeenth century offers a more fruitful line of investigation because of the presence of motets and even instrumental music in prints that are arranged for specific liturgical occasions – notably

Monteverdi's Vespers of 1610.[1] James Armstrong's detailed study of the texts set by Giovanni Francesco Anerio in his *Antiphonae, seu Sacrae Cantiones* of 1613, a book specifically destined for Vespers, led to some surprising conclusions. Of the fifty-nine sets of Vespers antiphons set by Anerio, only twelve are 'liturgically impeccable', that is, 'in the proper liturgical order without significant textual alterations'.[2] The other sets show various anomalies: the texts may be correct, but in a different order; the texts may be antiphons, but not for Vespers; the texts may be paraphrases of Vespers antiphons; the texts may be altered or expanded or even compiled from several antiphons. Finally, the texts may be taken from other liturgical categories, such as responsories and Benedictus antiphons. For some texts Armstrong could find no liturgical source at all. He concluded that[3]

Anerio's collection, in its arrangement and in its selection of texts, suggests a much broader interpretation of the term antiphon than has previously been offered in the study of seventeenth-century Vesper music. It is no longer possible to dismiss settings of texts (like those in Monteverdi's 1610 Vespers) that do not conform to the antiphons of the Roman Breviary. Often the Breviary is merely a point of departure for the composer, who alters the antiphons or adds additional text.

Judging from the motets of Treviso 29, Anerio's practice seems to have been standard in the sixteenth century.

The question then arises: how could Anerio's liturgically anomalous motets replace the prescribed Vesper antiphons? A possible answer is found in the *Caeremoniale Episcoporum* of Clement VIII, first published in 1600. It directs that each psalm is to be framed by its own antiphon, but 'if it is desired, at the end of each psalm, the antiphon can be repeated by the organ, provided that the same antiphon is repeated out loud by some mansionaries [members of the plainchant choir] or others so deputed. And if anyone should wish to sing with the organ, let him sing only that same antiphon'.[4] Extrapolating from

---

[1] James Armstrong reviews the literature on this problem in 'The *Antiphonae, seu Sacrae Cantiones* (1613) of Giovanni Francesco Anerio: A Liturgical Study', *Studien zur italienisch-deutschen Musikgeschichte*, 9, ed. Friedrich Lippmann (Analecta Musicologica, 14; Cologne, 1974), 89–150; see pp. 89–91.

[2] Armstrong, 'The *Antiphonae*', p. 107.

[3] Ibid., p. 146. A collection similar to Anerio's, but dating from the Jubilee Year 1650, is Giuseppe Giamberti's *Antiphonae et Motecta Festi Omnibus propria et communia iuxta formam Breviarii Romani* (Rome, 1650). The feasts have from one to nine settings each, and the texts are distinguished as antiphons or motets. For a list of the contents, see José M. Llorens, *Le Opere musicali della Cappella Giulia, I. Manoscritti e edizioni fino al '700* (Studi e Testi 265; Vatican City, 1971), pp. 248–54.

[4] '. . . si placuit, finito quolibet Psalmo, poterit Antiphona per organum repeti, dum tamen per aliquos Mansionarios, aut alios ad id deputatos eadem Antiphona clara voce repetatur. Et, si quis esset, qui cum organo cantare vellet, nihil aliud cantet, quam ipsam Antiphonam'; Armstrong, 'The *Antiphonae*', p. 90, n. 8, quoting from the 1670 edition, p. 140.

this exception, Armstrong suggests that Anerio's antiphons were intended to replace the repetition of the antiphon after the psalm; the liturgically proper antiphon could have been performed before the psalm.[5]

James Moore's investigation of the antiphon settings composed by Grandi, Rovetta and Cavalli for the Church of St Mark in the first half of the seventeenth century yielded similar results. He concluded that 'it is clear that no attempt was ever made to set all of the antiphons of a feast as a sequence or even to set them cumulatively over the years in various publications'.[6] But he found 'a much more significant body of motets on texts drawn from the Magnificat antiphons', and he too supposed that 'the plainchant antiphon after the Magnificat must have been replaced by a motet on a number of occasions'.[7]

The motets of Treviso 29 differ from Anerio's print and the Venetian works because they are assembled from many sources and represent the text choices of many composers, except for the contra-facta. Yet here also the tendency is to set antiphon texts, especially those for the Magnificat, and responsories. The manuscript gives no hint as to whether the motets were performed at Mass or at Vespers. We only know that at some point during services on a particular feast, a motet was sung.

The testimony of archival sources

Evidence for the performance of motets during liturgical services in the sixteenth century is more plentiful but widely scattered. It is mostly found in sources not usually consulted by musicologists in this connection. Anthony Cummings, in his recent investigation of the diaries of the Sistine Chapel (for the years 1534–61, 1594, 1616), found that the motet was sung 'in a comparatively small number of liturgical contexts', almost all of which 'identify the motet exclusively with the Mass, with the Offertory, Elevation, and Communion'.[8] Most of the references occur after 1555 and the main location, when one is specified, is during the Offertory.[9] Other references are to performance at the end of Mass after the 'Ite, missa est',[10] and during

[5] Ibid., p. 109.

[6] Moore, *Vespers at St. Mark's*, p. 148.

[7] Ibid., p. 180.

[8] Anthony M. Cummings, 'Toward an Interpretation of the Sixteenth-Century Motet', *Journal of the American Musicological Society*, 34 (1981), 43–59; p. 45.

[9] Ibid., p. 47. The unusually detailed notes in the 1616 diaries often name not only the composer but also the particular motet that was sung 'all'offertorio'; see p. 47, n. 15. Cummings observes that the texts of the motets are drawn from a wide variety of liturgical sources, but more often from the Office than the Mass (pp. 48–9).

[10] It is perhaps this occasion for which Giovanni Animuccia composed three motets for the Cappella Giulia 'secundo la forma del Concilio di Trento et de l'offitio novo',

the Elevation.[11] While motets sung during the Offertory or after Mass are likely to have been proper to the feast, those sung during the Elevation were probably on texts referring to the Blessed Sacrament, such as *O sacrum convivium*, *O salutaris hostia* and *Ave verum*.[12]

The Sistine diaries, according to Cummings, never link the motet with the Office, leading him to believe that 'types of music other than motets were appropriate to the celebration of the Office, presumably *alternatim* works exclusively in *falsobordone*'.[13] It is always risky to advance a position on the basis of negative evidence. If the diaries mention performance of motets occasionally, they do so only incidentally; this was not their purpose. To proceed on this basis to make conclusions about the function of motets in general is rash. Although Cummings realizes that his evidence 'does not account for significant differences in regional preference and practice',[14] it may not even be applicable outside the Papal Chapel. The papal ceremonies give much more emphasis to Mass than to the Office; the ceremonial of Paride de Grassis specifies that the full chapel (all members of the Curia as well as the singers) is required to participate in thirty-five Masses but in only ten Vesper services in the year – on Vigils of the principal feasts.[15] However, the singers themselves, according to the Constitutions, were to be present during all daily offices. Since it was the

specifying that they were to be sung 'quando passa il Papa'. For the excerpt from the payment accounts of 23 December 1568, see Richard Sherr, 'The Papal Chapel ca. 1492–1513 and its Polyphonic Sources' (Ph.D. diss., Princeton University, 1975), p. 182. Sherr notes that the three feasts for which the motets were written – the Vigil of Christmas, All Saints Day, and Ascension – were celebrated in St Peter's and suggests that the motets were 'placed either in the beginning of the service (during the processional) or at the end (during the recessional)' (ibid., p. 183).

[11] Cummings, 'Toward an Interpretation', pp. 51–2.

[12] *O sacrum convivium* is named twice in the 1594 diaries as the motet sung after Mass; ibid., p. 51. The practice of singing the antiphon *O sacrum convivium* during the Elevation dates back to at least 1450, when a Strasbourg statute prescribed it for certain occasions; see Joseph A. Jungmann, *The Mass of the Roman Rite*, transl. Frances A. Brunner (2 vols.; New York, 1951–5), 2, p. 216. Louis XII, in ill health during his later years, attributed his recovery in part to the 'miraculous effect' of the singing of the hymn *O salutaris hostia*, and he ordered it to be sung throughout his realm at High Mass during the Elevation; see Edward E. Lowinsky, *The Medici Codex of 1518* (Monuments of Renaissance Music, 3; Chicago, 1968), 43.

[13] Cummings, 'Toward an Interpretation', p. 53.

[14] Ibid. Cummings concedes that 'the Sistine Chapel was an exceptional institution in some respects', but he states that 'its practices served as a model for other Italian as well as Northern institutions. Indeed, a range of evidence from other Italian centers of musical patronage corroborates the inferences suggested by the entries in the Sistine diaries' (ibid., p. 54). He presents, however, evidence only for Florence, but refers to Thomas D. Culley's monograph, *Jesuits and Music: I, A Study of the Musicians connected with the German College in Rome during the 17th Century and of their Activities in Northern Europe* (Sources and Studies for the History of the Jesuits, 2; St Louis, 1970), as supporting the evidence of the Papal Chapel.

[15] See Richard Sherr, 'The Singers of the Papal Chapel and Liturgical Ceremonies in the Early Sixteenth Century: Some Documentary Evidence', *Rome in the Renaissance: The City and the Myth*, ed. P. A. Ramsey (Binghamton, 1982), Table I, p. 253.

custom, at least in 1545, to sing Nones, Vespers and Compline consecutively,[16] the inclusion of motets might have extended the length of the services unduly. The Constitutions of the Papal Chapel give no hint of polyphonic performance in any service except Matins of the Nativity; the first three antiphons of the first Nocturn are to be sung in counterpoint, as well as the first and eighth responsories.[17] 'In contrapuncto' seems to mean improvisation over a plainchant (which might include *falsobordone*) of the kind described by Tinctoris in his *Liber de arte contrapuncti*. The Papal Chapel distinguished between *contrapunctus* and *cantus figuratus*; candidates for the position of singer were formally examined on their ability to sing 'cantus figuratus' well and to sing 'contrapunctus' adequately, in addition to singing plainchant and sight reading.[18] One cannot conclude from this evidence, however, that motets were not sung during Vespers. In fact, the evidence of the manuscripts suggests otherwise (see below, pp. 30–31).

In other Roman churches, Vespers was celebrated with more circumstance. Giovanni Francesco Anerio's three-volume publication of antiphons is intended for Vespers and Compline and provides at least one motet, but usually four, for fifty-nine Vesper services. Anerio published his volume in 1613, the year he became *maestro di cappella* at Santa Maria dei Monte in Rome, a relatively small Jesuit church built in 1582.[19] To celebrate so many Vesper services with extended polyphony – some of the psalms, the Magnificat and the hymn may also have been performed polyphonically – indicates that the audience must have been different. I venture to guess that the class of people whose enthusiasm and financial support led to the great flourishing of art and music in the Netherlands, and especially in Antwerp, about which we are well informed[20] – the merchants, bankers and guild members – are the same ones who congregated in church after the day's work and heard Vespers. Such services must have been influenced by – and probably competed directly with – the *oratorio vespertino* of San Filippo Neri's Oratory, in which music, at first limited to *laude* framing sermons, gradually came to assume a

---

[16] Chapter 49 of the Constitutions, 'De Nonis, Vesperis et Completorio'; see Fr. X. Haberl, *Die römische "Schola cantorum" und die päpstlichen Kapellsänger bis zur Mitte des 16. Jahrhunderts* (Bausteine für Musikgeschichte, 3; Leipzig, 1888), p. 106.

[17] Chapter 64, 'De Matutino noctis Nativitatis Domini', ibid., pp. 107–8.

[18] Chapter 3, 'Modus examinis': 'primo considerandum est, si cantor examinandus habeat bonam et perfectam vocem; secundo, si cantet bene cantum figuratum; tertio si cantet sufficienter contrapunctum; quarto, si cantet cantum planum; quinto, si sciat bene legere'; ibid., p. 96.

[19] Armstrong, 'The *Antiphonae*', p. 92.

[20] See Edward E. Lowinsky, 'Music in the Culture of the Renaissance', *Renaissance Essays from the Journal of the History of Ideas*, ed. Paul Oskar Kristeller and Philip P. Wiener (Harper Torchbooks, New York and Evanston, 1968), pp. 337–81, esp. pp. 341–2. The Confraternity of Our Lady in Antwerp had its own chapel in the cathedral, with its own organ, organist, singers and instrumentalists.

central role. The *oratorio vespertino*, held outdoors in summer, indoors in winter, followed Vespers on Sundays and feast days.[21] The music was mostly strophic and set to Italian texts, but motets are included in some of the books of *laude* printed for the Oratory. Anerio's family was closely connected with Filippo Neri, and in 1619 Anerio wrote his *Teatro armonico spirituale di madrigali* for use in Neri's Oratory.[22] The *Teatro* includes a list of feasts of the winter season, with two or three madrigals for each.

In Venice the counterparts of the confraternities in the north and the oratories in Rome were the *scuole grandi*, the charitable organizations of laymen. They built their own magnificent halls and sometimes even churches. Music was an important part of their services, and the great *scuole* hired *cantadori* to sing in processions and on Sundays and major feasts. Jonathan Glixon, in his study of the Venetian *scuole grandi*, was able to find extensive material on musicians and their duties, but was constrained to admit that 'the most mysterious aspect of musical activities at the Scuole Grandi is the music itself. No actual music survives, and there is little documentary indication of what music was performed.'[23] We do know, however, that music was sung at Mass and Vespers and during processions.

The model for the musical life of the *scuole grandi* was, of course, St Mark's, with whose splendid endowment they could not hope to compete. The Duomo of Treviso, however, had the musical forces that enabled it to emulate the sumptuous ritual celebrations of its nearest neighbour and – always bearing in mind that St Mark's was a ducal chapel and not, at that time, a cathedral[24] – it is to Venice that we must look for evidence of when the motets of Treviso 29 were performed.

Thanks to the painstaking research of James Moore, we now know considerably more about the performance of polyphonic music in St Mark's. It is evident that Vespers was celebrated with far more circumstance at St Mark's than in the Papel Chapel; in 1515, for example, the singers had to be present at some two hundred Vesper services, and on all feasts of duplex rank they were expected to perform polyphony at one or both Vespers.[25] Attendance at Mass was required on the same days plus a few more. Commemorations of the

---

[21] On the *oratorio vespertino*, see Howard E. Smither, *A History of the Oratorio*, 1 (Chapel Hill, 1977), 51–7.

[22] Ibid., pp. 118–19.

[23] Jonathan Emmanuel Glixon, 'Music at the Venetian *Scuole Grandi* 1440–1540' (Ph.D. diss., Princeton University, 1979), 1, p. 188.

[24] St Mark's remained the private chapel of the Doge until 1807, when it became the Cathedral of Venice; see Moore, 'The *Vespero delli Cinque Laudate* and the Role of *Salmi Spezzati* at St. Mark's', *Journal of the American Musicological Society*, 34 (1981), 249–78; p. 254.

[25] Moore, *Vespers at St. Mark's*, pp. 183–4 and Appendix II, pp. 313–30. The list of 1515 was still valid in 1564, since it was copied into a *Ceremoniale* of that year; ibid., p. 183.

Virgin were prescribed 'for all days during Advent which do not contain feasts of double rank, and then are liberally sprinkled through the rest of the church year. . . . Commemorative motets occurred at the very end of Vespers, following the Magnificat.'[26] Although Moore dealt mainly with music of the seventeenth century, he drew on liturgical sources of St Mark's that date from the sixteenth century, the principal one being Bartolomeo Bonifacio's *Caeremoniale rituum sacrorum* of 1564, which is extant in five manuscript copies.[27]

Scattered throughout this meticulous description of the ceremonies at St Mark's by the *maestro delle ceremonie* are references to the performance of polyphonic music. Motets seem to have functioned regularly as a replacement for the *Deo gratias* at the end of Second Vespers: '. . . and after the singers have sung *Deo gratias* or while they sing a motet in place of *Deo gratias* . . .';[28] '. . . and when the motet of *Deo gratias* is sung, lights are hung above the altar . . . when the motet is finished, the singers' lectern is taken away'.[29] According to the ceremonial, 'the *Deo gratias* is always sung on every Sunday of the year at Mass and Vespers except during the Sundays of Lent, in which the *Ave Regina celorum* is sung at Compline'.[30]

There is one reference to the singing of motets at Mass, but from the wording this appears to be normal practice: 'On Carnival Thursday the singers sing the *Missa della bataglia* with the usual motets.'[31]

---

[26] Ibid., p. 153.

[27] Numbers 7–11 in the list of *Ceremoniali* in Moore, *Vespers*, pp. 69–70; for a description of Bonifacio's work, see pp. 71–3.

[28] '. . . et dicto per cantores deo gratias vel dum cantores dicunt motetum pro deo gratias . . .'; from the order of the ritual on the Feast of All Saints, when the Doge normally comes to the window to hear Vespers. I use the earliest of the five versions, Cod. Lat. III–172 (=2276) of the Biblioteca Nazionale Marciana, fol. 31v. For other references to the singing of motets at St Mark's, some drawn from Francesco Sansovino, *Venetia città nobilissima et singolare* (Venice, 1581, and later editions with added material), see David Douglas Bryant, 'Liturgy, Ceremonial and Sacred Music in Venice at the Time of the Counter-Reformation' (Ph.D. diss., King's College, University of London, 1981), p. 14.

[29] '. . . et quando se dice il mottetto del deo gratias se impizza la luminaria sopra l'altar . . .; finitto el mottetto, se tira via el lettorin di cantori'; from the ceremony for Vespers on the Vigil of the Nativity, ibid., fol. 57. The *Ceremoniale* is written partly in Latin and partly in the Venetian dialect. I take 'impizza' to be derived from *impiccare*. In another version of the ceremonial, the 'Cantores cantant Motetum pro Deo Gratias' during the Vigil of Epiphany at First Vespers; see Moore, *Vespers*, p. 360, n. 335.

[30] 'In omnibus dominicis diebus totius Anni in Missis et vesperis et semper cantant Deo gratias exceptis Dominicis quadragesime in quibus cantant ad Completorium Ave regina celorum' (ibid., fol. 46v). The same wording is found in the list of singers' obligations for the year 1515; see Moore, *Vespers*, p. 286. The response *Deo gratias* follows *Ite, missa est* or *Benedicamus Domino* at Mass and *Benedicamus Domino* at Vespers.

[31] 'El zorno della zuobba grassa si canta la Messa della bataglia da li cantori con li mottetti soliti' (Venice Lat. III–172 [=2276], fol. 57). This was probably Janequin's Mass, based on his famous chanson, *La Bataille de Marignan*. For references to the singing of motets in Giovanni Pace's Ceremonial of 1678, see Moore, *Vespers*, Documents 29, 120 and 121 on pp. 242 and 277. We know from a letter of Monteverdi that on days when

The plural form indicates that there were at least two motets performed. One was probably sung during the Offertory, as in the Papal Chapel, the other in response to *Ite, missa est*.[32] On at least one ceremonial occasion, the Feast of the Redeemer on the third Sunday in July, which is celebrated at the Church of the Redentore, a motet was performed by the singers of St Mark's at the Elevation as well.[33]

Further information about performance at St Mark's can be gleaned from the Acts of the Procurators in 1562, a time when the musical establishment was being reorganized into a *cappella piccola* and a *cappella grande*. The *cappella piccola* was to consist of six choirboys and two tenors and was to sing 'all'officio il Sanctus, Agnus Dei et post communionem della messa' and every Thursday and Friday 'una

---

the Most Holy Blood of Our Lord was displayed, the singers performed motets 'all day long'; see ibid., p. 184 and p. 363, n. 369. In 1761 the singers were still obliged to sing 'Mottetti tutto il giorno' on the same days; see ibid., Document 143, p. 302.

[32] The practice of singing polyphony in place of the *Deo gratias* is found in England as well as on the Continent; it goes back at least to the fourteenth century, when the custom was sanctioned by the Exeter Ordinal of Bishop John Grandisson of 1337; see Frank Ll. Harrison, *Music in Medieval Britain* (London, 1958), pp. 109–11 and, for later motet replacements, pp. 226–8. The tradition flourished in the sixteenth century and can be traced as far forward as the eighteenth century in the Papal Chapel.

Ten polyphonic settings of the *Deo gratias* are found in Treviso 10, a manuscript that also contains eighteen Magnificat settings and a set of polyphonic responses to prefaces. Except for the five-voice setting (fols. 6v–7) – ascribed to N. Olivetus in Treviso 3, fol. 40 – these are short settings for four voices, all anonymous. Another anonymous setting *a 5* occurs in Treviso 25, fol. 100. *Deo gratias* settings are also found in manuscripts of the Sistine Chapel: C.S. 44, fol. 101v (anon., *a 4*); C.S. 65, fol. 3v (anon., *a 4*); C.S. 272, fol. 17 (anon., *a 4*). The last two are seventeenth-century manuscripts. Four settings of *Deo dicamus gratias*, a response to *Benedicamus Domino* paraphrasing the plainchant, appear in C.S. 18, a manuscript entirely devoted to Festa's works; a modern edition may be found in *Costanzo Festa, Opera omnia*, I, ed. Alexander Main (Corpus mensurabilis musicae, 25; American Institute of Musicology, 1962), 105–8. As late as the eighteenth century the *Deo gratias* was still being sung polyphonically; see Cappella Giulia MS XV 29, which contains eight settings by various composers.

Tinctoris gives a five-part *Deo gratias* in his book on counterpoint as an example of *res facta*; the beginning of the Tenor resembles the *Ite missa est* melody of Mass IX for feasts of the Blessed Virgin (L.U. 43); see *Johannis Tinctoris Opera theoretica*, ed. Albert Seay, 2 (Corpus scriptorum de musica, 22; American Institute of Musicology, 1975), 107–10. A few settings of the *Deo gratias* are also found in northern sources: an anonymous setting *a 3* in Copenhagen, Det Kongelige Bibliotek, MS Ny Kongelige Samling 1848, 2°, p. 279; a troped setting by H. F[inck] in Berlin, Staatsbibliothek Preussischer Kulturbesitz, Mus. Ms. 40021, fol. 149v; Philippus de Wildre *a 12*, in Ulhard, *Concentus 8, 6, 5, 4 vocum* (RISM 1545²), no. 36; and, of course, the famous 36-voice canon *Deo gratia[s]* published by Petreius, *Tomus tertius psalmorum selectorum* (RISM 1542⁶), no. 40, which may be identical with the lost Ockeghem 36-voice motet; see Edward E. Lowinsky, 'Ockeghem's Canon for Thirty-Six Voices: An Essay in Musical Iconography', *Essays in Musicology in Honor of Dragan Plamenac*, ed. Gustave Reese and Robert J. Snow (Pittsburgh, 1969), pp. 155–80.

[33] 'co' motetti cantati da i Musici di San Marco all'Offertorio, & alla Levatione'; the report comes from the 1604 edition of Sansovino's *Venetia città nobilissima*, fol. 336v, and is cited in Bryant, 'Liturgy, Ceremonial and Sacred Music', pp. 14 and 93.

messa grande et similmente li vesperi'. Moreover, whenever the Doge came to services and on all solemn feast days and vigils, the *cappella piccola* was to join with the *cappella grande*, and on Saturdays at High Mass both chapels were to sing 'uno moteto all'offertorio'.[34]

Recently, James Moore has discovered a Venetian document of 1639 concerning the performance of motets during services. The *Provveditori di Commun* ordered that in the *scuole*, music set to 'texts with made-up words which are not found in holy books' could be sung only 'during the Offertory, and the Elevation, and after the Agnus Dei, and similarly between the psalms at Vespers'.[35] This regulation evidently came about in response to the decree of the Patriarch Giovanni Tiepolo in 1628 that 'in the music performed in their churches, oratories and chapels, no words are to be sung but those from the Holy Scriptures allowed by the Holy Roman Catholic Church, which should follow one after the other as they appear in the text itself, without transpositions in their order or the interpolation of words gathered from different sections of Holy Scripture, Breviaries or Missals'.[36] The Patriarch's warning seems to reflect a situation that had got out of hand; although the document does not say so explicitly, the inference is that these motets with centonate texts (that is, with fragments gathered from different sources) were being used to replace rather than to supplement liturgical chants. The loophole granted by the *Provveditori di Commun* applies to those places in the service where motets could be sung in addition to the proper liturgical text; it recalls the licence granted by the *Caeremoniale Episcoporum* to give the repetition of the psalm antiphon at Vespers to the organ (see above, p. 20 and n. 4).[37]

The problem of accommodating polyphonic music in a liturgy traditionally tied to plainchant is one that has occupied the ecclesiastical hierarchy for centuries and even been the subject of a papal bull, John XXII's *Docta sanctorum* of 1324–5. He deplored the new music, with its measured time, hockets and added voices in many notes, and

---

[34] The document is published in René Lenaerts, 'La Chapelle de Saint-Marc à Venise sous Adriaen Willaert (1527–1562). Documents inédits', *Bulletin de l'Institut Historique belge de Rome*, 19 (1938), 205–55; see pp. 242–3.

[35] Moore, *Vespers at St. Mark's*, p. 152.

[36] As quoted by Moore, ibid., p. 151.

[37] The regulations of the *Caeremoniale Episcoporum* still figure in the Motu Proprio on Sacred Music of Pius X of 1903: 'As the texts that may be rendered in music, and the order in which they are to be rendered, are determined for every liturgical function, it is not lawful to confuse this order or to change the prescribed texts for others selected at will, or to omit them either entirely or even in part, unless when the rubrics allow that some versicles of the text be supplied with the organ, while these versicles are simply recited in the choir. However it is permissible, according to the custom of the Roman Church, to sing a motet to the Blessed Sacrament after the *Benedictus* in a Solemn Mass. It is also permitted, after the Offertory prescribed for the Mass has been sung, to execute during the time that remains a brief motet to words approved by the Church'. See *Motu Proprio of Pope Pius X and Other Papal Documents on Liturgical Music* (Catholic Education Press, n.p., 1928), p. 9.

censured the singers who 'intoxicate the ear without satisfying it' and create 'a sensuous and indecent atmosphere'; at most he was willing to allow, on solemn feasts, a simple counterpoint over the chant.[38] Two centuries later, when the Cardinals discussed sacred music at the Council of Trent, it was again mainly the character of the polyphonic music to which they objected,[39] and the proscription of profane music was voted by the Council on 17 September 1562. However, there was a faction that was disturbed by the unintelligibility of the liturgical texts, whether spoken or sung. For the session of 19 September 1562 on the abuses of the Mass, a committee of deputies prepared a proposal for reform in which priests were enjoined to 'pronounce the words fittingly, distinctly, and gravely, so that simultaneously the words may be understood and listeners aroused to piety', and 'if anything is to be sung with the organ from the sacred services while they are in progress, let it be recited in a simple clear voice beforehand so that no one will miss any part of the eternal reading of the sacred writings'.[40] The committee was influenced by a letter that the Bishop of Vienna, Federicus Nausea, had sent to Paul III in June 1543 with a number of suggestions for the

---

[38] Ibid., pp. 35–7.

[39] See Karl Weinmann, *Das Konzil von Trent und die Kirchenmusik* (Leipzig, 1919), p. 4. The *Missa della Bataglia* was a prime target. In discussing the abuses during Mass at the session of 8 August 1562, the question was raised whether music 'which delights the ear more than the mind and which is seen to excite the faithful to lascivious rather than to religious thoughts, should be taken away from the Masses. For in this type of music profane things are often sung, as for example that of the hunt (*caccia*) and the battle (*battaglia*)'; see Robert S. Hayburn, *Papal Legislation on Sacred Music 95 A.D. to 1977 A.D.* (Collegeville, Minn., 1979), p. 27. The charge of performing lascivious and impure music was also levelled at the organists. Various church councils and synods of the fifteenth and sixteenth centuries attempted to deal with this problem; for excerpts from the records, see K. G. Fellerer, 'Church Music and the Council of Trent', *The Musical Quarterly*, 39 (1953), 576–94, esp. 577–81.

The extent to which organ or instrumental music had come to replace Gregorian chant is made graphically clear in a document of 1560 from Valencia Cathedral. To assist the polyphonic choir, which consisted of only four singers and six choirboys, the archbishop created an ensemble of four instrumentalists who played 'chirimies, sacabuig, flautes, cornetes, orlos e trompon' (shawms, sackbut, flutes or recorders, cornetti, crumhorns and trombone). They were obliged to perform in both Vespers on solemn feasts 'at the end of each psalm, at the end of the hymn, at the end of the Magnificat, and at the end of the episcopal benediction'. At solemn Masses they played the Kyrie in place of the organ, and performed at the Offertory 'si los cantors no diran algun motet', at the Agnus, and after the episcopal benediction. They were also to play at Salve services 'als gaudes y apres del motet', to alternate with the organ and the singers in 'les salves solemnes' and to perform 'apres del motet' (the document is written in Catalán). Naturally, they accompanied the Te Deum and the entries of the king and archbishop, and they took part in all processions. See José Climent, 'La capilla de música de la catedral de Valencia', *Anuario musical*, 37 (1982), 55–69; see pp. 61–5. Two years later, the number of singers was doubled (ibid., pp. 61–2), and by 1580 the number of instrumentalists had grown to eight (ibid., p. 65).

[40] See Hayburn, *Papal Legislation on Sacred Music*, p. 27.

future Council, including the reform of church music. He charged singers with five abuses, among which was the following:[41]

Nor do they recognize the fact that all too often those things which are prescribed for the sacred services are omitted or cut short for the sake of the harmonies of songs or organ music. These parts consist of the Prophecies, the Epistles, the *Credo*, the Preface, the actions of graces, the prayers, and other things of that sort which are of great importance.

In the end, only a general decree concerning music was issued by the Council, and the specific regulation of music in divine services was left to provincial councils and synods. None of the documents emanating from the Council discusses the problem of motets usurping the place of liturgical chant. This may be because motets, as Paolo Cortese remarked early in the century, were considered to be 'supernumerary and ingrafted',[42] that is, as paraliturgical ornaments to the service.

The evidence of church choirbooks

There is yet a third type of evidence for the use of motets in liturgical services that has largely been overlooked, and that is the arrangement of compositions in church choirbooks. These books are usually devoted to a single genre – Masses, motets, lamentations, hymns, psalms, Magnificats. This is generally the case with the Treviso choirbooks; only a few contain more than one genre: MSS 3 and 18 had hymns, antiphons and Magnificats, MS 12 psalms and Magnificats, MS 25 hymns and antiphons. In the Sistine Chapel, however, there are a number of choirbooks from the sixteenth century in which Masses and motets co-exist and several in which hymns, Magnificats and motets are found together. This suggests that the manuscripts were made up to meet the needs of particular services: those combining Masses and motets for the celebration of Mass, those containing hymns, Magnificats and psalms for Vespers or Compline. Such an arrangement makes sense in view of the size of these choirbooks, in which a page averages 500 × 360 mm; they are not too large to be lifted by one person, but it would be awkward to exchange them during services. The task of carrying the choirbooks was divided between the two newest singers; to the last singer hired fell the duty of removing the choirbook from its stand, to the other singer the obligation to place it there.[43] The choirbook must have

---

[41] Ibid., p. 26.

[42] Paolo Cortese, *De cardinalatu libri tres* (Castel Cortesiano, 1510), as translated by Nino Pirrotta in 'Music and Cultural Tendencies in 15th-Century Italy', *Journal of the American Musicological Society*, 19 (1966), 127–61; see p. 154.

[43] 'Ad ultimum cantorem pertinet amovere libros et ad penultimum cantorem ipsos

stayed on the lectern throughout the service. Therefore, if we find motets in a Mass manuscript, it is likely that they were sung during Mass, and if motets appear in a choirbook together with hymns, Magnificats or psalms, they were probably sung during Vespers or Compline.

Considered from this point of view, the Sistine manuscripts destined for Mass reveal some interesting facets. The Masses always come first. For example, C.S. 16 has ten Masses followed by five motets, C.S. 17 six Masses and five motets, C.S. 19 six Masses and nine motets. The motets in Mass manuscripts tend to be among the most brilliant examples of the genre, often in five and six voices. C.S. 16, assembled during the pontificate of Leo X, contains six Masses for four voices (by Brumel, Josquin, Févin and Penet), three for five voices (by Pipelare, Févin and Mouton), and one for six voices (Willaert). The motet section contains one work by Regis, *Clangat plebs flores a 5*, and four by Josquin: *Benedicta es celorum regina a 6, Praeter rerum seriem a 6, Memor esto verbi tui a 4*, and *Virgo salutiferi a 5*. There can be no doubt that the choice of works reflects the musical predilections of Leo X, and that the choirbook was probably used at the most solemn papal Masses. C.S. 17, assembled during the pontificate of Paul III, has three Masses for four voices (by Richafort, Claudin and Gascongne), two for five (by Hesdin and Morales) and one for six (by Morales). The five motets, by Morales, Fremin, Maitre Jhan, Jachet and Festa, are all settings of Marian antiphons for five and six voices. This choirbook was most probably used for high Mass on feast days of the Virgin. C.S. 19, likewise from the pontificate of Paul III, has three Masses for four voices (by Beausseron, Gascongne and Lupi), and three for five voices (by Morales, Pieton and Hesdin). Four of the nine motets (by Beausseron, Lhéritier, Brumen, Arcadelt, Maitre Jhan, [Willaert], Josquin and Morales) are on Marian texts, appropriate to three of the Masses: two *Missae de Beata Virgine*, and a *Missa Benedicta es coelorum regina*. Other sixteenth-century manuscripts showing a similar arrangement of Masses and motets are: C.S. 13, 26, 45, 55 and 57.[44] The two fifteenth-century manuscripts of Masses and motets, C.S. 35 and 63, do not follow this arrangement; the motets seem to be entered at random between the Masses. However, this may be due to the way in which the manuscripts were put together; motets may have been added on blank openings.

Sistine choirbooks appropriate to Vespers or Compline and containing motets are C.S. 15, 18, 29 and 44. There are considerably

---

situare in legio seu facistorio'; from Chapter XV of the 1545 Constitutions of the Papal Chapel; see Haberl, *Die römische "Schola cantorum"*, p. 99.

[44] The Sistine Chapel also possessed Alonso Lobo's *Liber primus missarum* (Madrid, 1602), which contains six Masses and seven 'moteta devotione inter missarum solemnia decantanda'; see Josephus M. Llorens, *Capellae Sixtinae Codices musicis notis instructi sive manu scripti sive praelo excussi* (Studi e Testi, 202; Vatican City, 1960), pp. 184–5.

fewer of these, and the reason is probably that there were fewer papal Vespers than papal Masses (see above, p. 22).

The performance of motets in Treviso Cathedral

The Ordinal of Clemens a Stadiis for Treviso Cathedral, unlike that of Bonifacio for St Mark's, comprises only a listing of the prescribed chants for each service of the church calendar; it tells us nothing about performance. But given the similarities of the liturgy of Treviso to that of St Mark's, it is likely that performance practices were also similar. Throughout the century polyphonic music played a prominent role in the cathedral's services. When Giovanni di Liegi became choirmaster in 1504, he had to promise the chapter to copy for the cathedral every year a repertory of four Masses, six Magnificats and eight motets 'from the compositions of the most outstanding men'. These compositions had to be first rehearsed and then approved by choirmaster and singers.[45] While similar documents do not exist for later choirmasters, it is likely that they had to fulfil the same conditions, and the hands found in the Treviso choirbooks may well be those of the choirmasters themselves. On his death in 1574, Liberale Sugana, a singer since 1536 and later choirmaster, left to the cathedral a number of volumes of Masses, psalms, hymns, antiphons and motets that he had copied himself.[46] In 1527 Francesco Santacroce received 93 *lire* for copying a choirbook, and in 1574 six books of motets transcribed by him were rebound.[47] Many of the choirmasters also composed for the cathedral's services; we have Vespers and Compline settings by Nasco and by Santacroce,[48] in addition to numerous other works in the Treviso choirbooks. Vespers was probably celebrated with great solemnity, following the practice of St Mark's. The liturgical calendar, with its large number of duplex feasts, supports this likelihood.

There is one aspect of Treviso 29 that has a bearing on performance and that raises a question as to who sang from it. Church singers normally sang from choirbooks large enough to be seen by as many as twenty singers at once. But Treviso 29 is a set of part-books. This makes it likely that only a few singers read from each part. These

---

[45] D'Alessi, *La Cappella musicale*, pp. 59–60 and Doc. 8, pp. 229–30.

[46] Ibid., p. 122 and Doc. 19, p. 243. The notice comes from the cathedral's Necrology, where mention is made of the 'diversa musicae artificialis tam Missarum quam psalmorum, hymnorum, antiphonarum et Motectorum volumina propriis manibus conscripta'. Note that a differentiation is made between antiphons and motets – a distinction that may also be found in fifteenth-century sources, such as ModB; see Charles E. Hamm, *A Chronology of the Works of Guillaume Dufay Based on a Study of Mensural Practice* (Princeton, 1964), p. XI.

[47] D'Alessi, *La Cappella musicale*, p. 178.

[48] Ibid., pp. 108, 116 and 86–8. For other references to polyphonic Vesper services, see pp. 120–1, 233, 242.

singers were probably Varisco himself and a group of highly skilled performers. They may have sung at Mass or at Vespers at a time when the church choir did not regularly perform. (Unfortunately, any records of the singers' duties that may have existed are now lost.) They may also have sung during processions, although a music book containing 175 motets would not be easy to carry and sing from.[49] But there is also another possibility: there were in Treviso confraternities like those of the Venetian *scuole*. The Confraternity of St Liberalis, the patron of the city of Treviso, was founded in the Duomo in 1360. In 1532 Zanin Bisan, a singer in the cathedral and official of the confraternity, petitioned the chapter for funds to mount the usual 'reppresentatione' on the feast of St Liberalis.[50] Pietro Varisco was an official of this confraternity for some time during the period 1564–77.[51] A second confraternity was founded in the Duomo in 1496, the Scuola del Sacratissimo Corpo de Christo, for which the cathedral's singers supplied the music. It was from a description of one of their services in 1524 that D'Alessi discovered the 'Precursors of Adriano Willaert in the Practice of *Coro Spezzato*', to cite the title of his article on the subject.[52] In particular, the choir performed 'in canto figurato . . . uno vespero et . . . una messa' on 3 November in commemoration of the deceased members of the confraternity.[53] There was also a third confraternity, the Scuola dell'Annunziata, to which Nicolò Olivetto, *maestro di cappella* at the Duomo, belonged in 1529.[54]

Pietro Varisco's anthology, with its heavy emphasis on saints' days and absence of major feasts such as Easter, Ascension, Pentecost and Corpus Christi, may well have served for one of these confraternities, and probably the one to which he belonged, the Confraternity of St Liberalis. Singers and instrumentalists were accepted as members, free of dues, as early as the fourteenth century; one may therefore assume that music played a significant role in the services.[55] The *mariegola* (the official record book) of the confraternity specifies the following services under the statutes of 1365:[56]

---

[49] We do know that the singers regularly sang litanies in polyphony during processions. In 1524 the canons protested to the bishop about the scandalous behaviour of the choirmaster Francesco Santacroce, who stubbornly refused to follow the custom of singing 'le litanie in canto figurato' when returning on general processions; see ibid., Document 10, pp. 231–2.

[50] Ibid., p. 29 and n. 3.

[51] See Liberali, *Lo stato personale del clero* (See Chapter 2, n. 2 above), p. 33. Liberali's documentary study stops at 1577, but Varisco was probably a lifetime member of the Confraternity.

[52] In *Journal of the American Musicological Society*, 5 (1952), 187–210.

[53] D'Alessi, *La Cappella musicale*, p. 124.

[54] Ibid., p. 90.

[55] Ibid., p. 30.

[56] '. . . qualibet dominica tercia cuiuslibet mensis celebrari debeat missa una solemnis in honorem et super altare sancti Liberalis ubi corpus eius in pace sepultum felicissime requiescit. . . . Missa una in honorem beatissimi ac gloriosissimi confessoris

every third Sunday of each month shall be celebrated a solemn Mass in honour of and upon the altar of St Liberalis, where his body, buried in peace, happily rests.

. . . every fourth Sunday of each month a Mass in honour of the most blessed and glorious confessor Liberalis is to be solemnly celebrated and on the Monday following a Mass for all the souls of deceased brothers and sisters and benefactors.

. . . eight days after the feast of the holy and most glorious confessor Liberalis a general Mass for the souls of all brothers and sisters of the said school shall be solemnly celebrated.

By the fifteenth century these feasts were surely ornamented with polyphonic song, and by Varisco's time the confraternity may have expanded its religious devotions to all major feast days (the last entries in the *mariegola* are dated 1513; they add nothing new to the statutes of 1365 insofar as religious ceremonies are concerned).

Liberalis qualibet dominica quarta mensis cuiuslibet celebratur solemniter ita et die lune immediate sequenti una missa pro animabus omnium confratrum et sororum ac benefactorum defunctorum. . . . Infra dies octo proxime venturos post festum sancti ac gloriosissimi confessoris Liberalis una missa generalis pro animabus omnium confratrum et sororum dicte schole solemniter celebretur'. D'Alessi's knowledge of the confraternity came from an eighteenth-century manuscript compendium. I was fortunate enough to find the originals of two *mariegole* in the Archivio di Stato, Venice (Scuole piccole, B. 396bis). The citations are found on fols. 18v, 21 and 22 of the second book, copied in the late fifteenth or early sixteenth century. The statutes are preceded by a life of St Liberalis.

4
Sources and Physical Description of the Manuscripts

MS 29: sources

Because Treviso 29 no longer exists, except for the incipits of texts and music left us by Mgr Giovanni D'Alessi, it is difficult to determine the sources from which Varisco compiled his anthology. In many cases, however, they can be surmised with a fair degree of probability. For example, MS 29 contains twenty motets by Palestrina. Nine of these (nos. 27, 38, 70, 82, 84, 104, 111, and II/32 and 33) can be found in *Johannis Petraloysii Praenestini Motettorum quae partim quinis, partim senis, partim octonis vocibus concinantur. Liber Secundus* (Venice: H. Scotto, 1572), and the remaining eleven (nos. 74, 76, 100, 107, 126–32) in the *Liber tertius* (Venice: H. Scotto, 1575). The chapter of Treviso owned the 1577 reprint of the first volume and the 1575 edition of the second volume.[1] If Varisco copied the motets from the books in the chapter's possession, the dates of MS 29 can be narrowed to between 1577 and 1584, his death date. At any rate, 1575 would be the earliest likely date for the beginning of the compilation. Other major sources (with six or more motets) are *Adriani Wilaert . . . musicorum sex vocum* (Gardane; RISM 1542[10]) with six motets (nos. 48, 69, and II/6, 8, 14, 28), *Musica quinque vocum que materna lingua moteta vocantur* (Gardane; RISM 1549[6]) with nine motets (nos. 2, 103, 124, and II/9, 13, 18, 23, 25, 27 – comprising every Marian motet in the print), and *Il terzo libro di motetti a cinque voci di Cipriano de Rore et de altri eccellentissimi musici* (Gardane; RISM 1549[8]) with six (nos. 75, 90, 116, 119, and II/7 and 20 – Varisco omitted works by northern composers who never worked in Italy). These are the major anthologies. Varisco also drew heavily on prints of individual composers:

> Bartholomeus Comes Gallicus, *Motetta quinque vocibus* (Gardane, 1547) (nos. 12, 14, 47, 53, 61, 110, 125, II/15)

[1] D'Alessi, *La Cappella musicale*, p. 198.

Johannes Continus, *Modulationum quinque vocum liber primus* (Scotto, 1560) (nos. 36, 40, 42, 49, 51, 60, 63, 66, 68, 72, 78, 80, 81, 85, 94, 112) and *Liber secundus* (Scotto, 1560) (nos. 54, 83, 98, 105, 118, II/43)

Nicolas Gombert, *Motectorum quinque vocum liber secundus* (Scotto, 1541 or 1550, or Gardane, 1552)[2] (nos. 37, 45, 77, 101, 113, 122, II/42)

Orlando di Lasso, *Sacrae cantiones . . . quinque vocum . . . liber primus* (Gardane, 1562) (nos. 86, 87, 93, 95, 102, 106)

Dominicus Phinot, *Liber primus mutetarum quinque vocum* (Gardane, 1552)[3] (nos. 4, 9, 13, 24, 62, 64, 108, II/19)

Francesco Portinaro, *Primi frutti . . . de motetti a cinque voci . . . Libro primo* (Gardane, 1548) (nos. 91, 109, 115, II/5, 21, 41)

Cipriano de Rore, *Motetta . . . quinque vocum* (Gardane, 1545) (nos. 43, 79, 88, 96, 121, 123, II/4, 12 – all except one of the nine motets ascribed to Rore in Treviso MS 29)

Adrian Willaert, *Musica nova* (Gardano, 1559) (nos. 32, 41, 57, 59, II/35–40 – all of the Marian motets except *Mittit ad virginem*)

Gioseffo Zarlino, *Quinque vocum moduli motecta vulgo nuncupata. Liber primus* (Gardane, 1549) (nos. 21, 99, 114, II/10, 26)

Probable sources for the other motets are listed in the Inventory below.

Striking is the number of prints issued from the presses of Gardane, many of them twenty and thirty years before Varisco started compiling his anthology. This suggests either that Gardane printed large runs or that he reprinted volumes without changing the dates.[4] Treviso 29 underlines the lengthy lifespan of sixteenth-

---

[2] The source is probably Scotto because of the spelling of the composer's name as Gomberth; Gardane spells it Gombert. Moreover, no. 113 is found only in Scotto's editions. However, Varisco must also have known Gardane's reprint, for it contains nos. 77 and 122, not in Scotto's editions.

[3] The same motets occur in the 1547 Lyons print of Phinot's motets, but Gardane is Varisco's source, as will be shown below.

[4] Mary S. Lewis has estimated Gardane's production to run from ca. 500 copies for subsidized editions of minor composers to 1250 or more for 'works of particularly popular composers of international appeal'; see 'Antonio Gardane and his Publications of Sacred Music, 1538–55' (Ph.D. diss., Brandeis University, 1979), p. 168. Gardane seems not to have made a general practice of reprinting volumes without changing the date, as did Susato. For exceptions to this policy, mostly involving single gatherings or pages, see ibid., pp. 264–74. (On Susato's reprints, see Kristine Karen Forney, 'Tielman Susato, Sixteenth-Century Music Printer: An Archival and Typographical Investigation' [Ph.D. diss., University of Kentucky, 1978], Chapter VI. Ute Meissner, *Der Antwerpener Notendrucker Tylman Susato* [2 vols.; Berliner Studien zur Musikwissenschaft, 11; Berlin, 1967], was aware of the problem [see 1, pp. 67–79], but did not approach it with the necessary bibliographical analysis.)

century motets. The generation of Josquin and Mouton is no longer represented, but their immediate successors – Gombert, Jachet, Maitre Jhan and Willaert – are among the mainstays. Mary S. Lewis, in discussing a group of 'ghost editions' from 1564 (by Gombert, Phinot, Pionnier and Porta) known only from the 1591 Gardano catalogue, found 'the thought of Gombert's motets gathering dust in the Gardano bookshop for forty years . . . somewhat surprising', and 'even a thirty-year lapse between publication and sale seems remarkable enough'.[5] The presence of motets by Gombert and Phinot and others of their generation in Treviso 29 challenges the suggestion that 'their popularity waned soon after mid-century'.[6]

Although Varisco demonstrably took many of his motets from printed sources, there are a few that seem not to have appeared in print, among them two by Willaert, *O proles Hispaniae* (no. 33) and *Sancte Francisce* (no. 56). Both occur in a central Willaert source, Wolfenbüttel, Herzog August Bibliothek, MS Guelf 293, and in Lucca, Biblioteca Statale, MS 775, copied in a northern hand. *O proles Hispaniae* is also found in Modena, Biblioteca Estense, MS C 314, another important Willaert source. Varisco must have had access to a manuscript that no longer exists, perhaps one of Willaert's own books that his nephew took back to Flanders after the master's death; Alvise made a stop in Treviso, where the scribe of MS 13 copied out a hymn 'zoso de li libri del ditto messer Adrian' on 24 June 1563.[7] I have found no concordances for Jachet Berchem's *Gaude et laetare* (II/34), Scaffen's *Senex puerum portabat* (no. 10) and Alberti's *Hic est dies egregius* (no. 23), probably a contrafactum, since it is addressed to the patron saint of Treviso, St Liberalis. One of the Nasco motets, *Inviolata* (no. II/1), and Spalenza's *Deus alma spes* (no. 71) likewise are unica, but Varisco could have obtained the music from the composers personally; both were active in Treviso during his lifetime (see below, pp. 52–55).

Fifteen of the motets in Treviso 29 have concordances in the cathedral's choirbooks: nos. 46, 48, 52, 63, 69 and 73 in MS 4; nos. 28, 40, 58 and 116 in MS 5; nos. 21 and 39 in MS 6; no. 34 in MS 7, and nos. 18 and 92 in MS 8. For nos. 34, 52, 58 and 92 the Treviso concordances are the only ones known. These duplications support the thesis that MS 29 was not intended for the cathedral, or at least not at services at the main altar where choirbooks would normally be used.

---

[5] Lewis, 'Antonio Gardane', p. 269.

[6] Ibid. As late as 1568 the Papal Chapel was singing motets and Masses by Mouton, Compère, Pipelare and Festa, as we know from the diary of Giovanni Antonio Merlo; see Richard Sherr, 'From the Diary of a 16th-Century Papal Singer', *Current Musicology*, 26 (1978), 83–98; see pp. 91–4. Sherr notes that music by Mouton and Festa was still being copied in 1563 (ibid., p. 98, n. 38). Motets by Festa and Josquin were sung 'all'offertorio' in the Papal Chapel in 1616; see Cummings, 'Toward an Interpretation', p. 47, n. 15.

[7] See D'Alessi, *La Cappella musicale*, p. 119.

The repertory of MS 30

Treviso 29 seems to have a close relationship with Treviso 30, another lost manuscript, which contained thirty-eight motets and two Masses for five and six voices (see the Inventory below). Treviso 30 appears to have been the source from which at least four of the seven motets were copied, for two reasons: 1) it is the only concordant source for nos. 1, 5, 29 and 55 (it may also be the source for no. II/22, Portinaro's *Benedicta et venerabilis*, although this motet also occurs in a Portinaro print of 1568); 2) it has the original versions of two motets that have contrafactum texts in MS 29. No. 8 of MS 29, Arcadelt's *Diem festum*, was discovered to be a contrafactum of *Signum salutis*, attributed in other sources to Crecquillon (see Inventory); in Treviso 30 it is ascribed to 'Archadelt'. No. 29, Testore's *In ferventis olei*, would not have been unmasked as a contrafactum were it not for its presence in Treviso 30 with the text *Domine ante te*. According to D'Alessi's thematic catalogue, the following note appeared at the end of the Bassus part-book: 'Ad clarissimum Jo. Baptistam Contarenum patavii praetorem dignissimum Guglielmus Textoris carceratus.' Testore was a French singer who was hired as a contralto at Padua Cathedral on 25 October 1557, where he served until at least 1566. From there he went to the court chapel in Mantua, where he is last recorded in 1571. He was the composer of two Masses and a book of madrigals.[8] His motet must be a musical plea directed to Giovanni Battista Contarini, a Paduan judge, to be released from jail. We know nothing more about his scrape with the law or about his career.

The repertory of MS 30 is similar to that of MS 29: a mixture of works by well-known authors such as Rore, Willaert, Morales, Jachet and Maitre Jhan; motets by composers who worked in Treviso (Santacroce, Nasco), and single works by Scaffen, Arcadelt, Innocenzo Alberti, Contino and Danckerts. Of authors not represented in MS 29 it has single works by composers of an earlier generation – Josquin, Lupus (actually Richafort) and Bauldeweyn – one motet each by Ruffo, Metallo, and Matthias (Werrecorre), and two works by otherwise unknown composers, Giuston and Cuglias (see the Inventory below). The presence of the Testore motet and four motets and a Mass by Franceso Portinaro may indicate a connection with Padua. One of them is an occasional motet in honour of 'Enrico

---

[8] On his Paduan career, see Raffaele Casimiri, 'Musica e musicisti nella Cattedrale di Padova nei sec. XIV, XV, XVI. Contributo per una storia', *Note d'Archivio per la Storia Musicale*, 18 (1941), 206, 207, 210, 212, and 19 (1942), 50 and 52. These notices escaped the attention of Pierre M. Tagmann, 'Testori, Guglielmo', *The New Grove Dictionary*, 18 (1980), 707, who gives only the employment at Mantua. Part of a letter from Testore to Duke Guglielmo Gonzaga concerning two singers of the Cardinal of Ferrara is printed in Iain Fenlon, *Music and Patronage in Sixteenth-Century Mantua*, 1 (Cambridge, 1980), 188, Doc. 45. The madrigal print of 1566 must predate his service in Mantua, since Testore's position is not given in the title; it is dedicated to Jacopo Pinsonio and dated Venice, 1 April 1566.

Brunesvic',[9] according to D'Alessi's note (see Inventory, no. II/1). None of the motets seems to be a contrafactum, and the pieces are not entered in liturgical order. Like MS 29, MS 30 was a set of part-books; the *Sexta pars* was missing before the manuscript was destroyed in 1944.[10] A further connection between the two manuscripts is the *Antoni pater inclite* (no. 5 in MS 29) ascribed to Morales but not known from any other source. In MS 30 the piece was originally anonymous; the name Morales, according to D'Alessi's card catalogue, was added in a later hand – perhaps after the concordance in MS 29.

In contradistinction to MS 29, none of the motets has a concordance in anthologies printed by Gardane, nor do the contents of MS 30 seem to have been widely circulated. Half the works are either unica or found exclusively in Trevisan sources. Not all of these are by local composers. Some of the unica may have had concordances in sources missing today; this seems likely in the case of the Scaffen motets in MSS 29 and 30. Eitner cited two books of motets for five voices published by Scotto in 1564 that were in the library at Celle; they are not listed in RISM.[11]

More difficult to explain is the presence of two motets by Rore, one an unicum, *Si resurrexistis* (no. 15), the other found elsewhere only in the sumptuous Munich codex of Rore's motets, *Pater noster* (no. 8). Rore's music was in great demand, and Gardane published three books of motets largely devoted to his works in the 1540s. Some of his compositions, however, were undertaken as gifts or commissions,[12] and we know how jealously some sixteenth-century patrons guarded 'their' motets and madrigals.[13] A number of these may not have entered the public domain. Alfonso d'Este had to go to extraordinary lengths first to obtain the 'buried treasure' of Willaert's *Musica nova* motets and madrigals from Polisena Pecorina and then to keep others from printing any of them before his ten-year privilege expired.[14] Up until now, some twenty-two of Rore's seventy-eight motets were known only from manuscript sources.[15] From this list we

[9] He was possibly Heinrich the Younger, Duke of Brunswick (Braunschweig) from 1514 to 1568, whose residence was in Wolfenbüttel, although he seems to have had little interest in music or time for it, having been engaged in wars throughout his reign; see Martin Ruhnke, *Beiträge zu einer Geschichte der deutschen Hofmusikkollegien im 16. Jahrhundert* (Berlin, 1963), pp. 16–22.

[10] See D'Alessi, *La Cappella musicale*, p. 185.

[11] Robert Eitner, *Biographisch-bibliographisches Quellen-Lexikon*, 8, p. 444. No sources from Celle are given in either series of RISM.

[12] On madrigals written by Rore for Ruberto Strozzi in the 1540s, see Richard J. Agee, 'Ruberto Strozzi and the Early Madrigal', *Journal of the American Musicological Society*, 36 (1983), 1–17; see pp. 12–16.

[13] One of the letters published by Agee confirms Antonfrancesco Doni's remarks about Neri Capponi's well-known zeal in keeping his compositions to himself; ibid., p. 13; on Capponi, see pp. 7–8.

[14] See Anthony Newcomb, 'Editions of Willaert's *Musica nova*: New Evidence, New Speculations', *Journal of the American Musicological Society*, 26 (1973), 132–45.

[15] See the catalogue in Jessie Ann Owens, 'An Illuminated Manuscript of Motets by

can subtract the eight hitherto unique motets of Treviso MS 29, all of which are contrafacta and were taken from the 1545 Gardane print. Still, it is likely that many Rore manuscripts have disappeared, for few have survived from his main centres of work, Ferrara, Venice and Parma. Treviso 30 shares concordances with three manuscripts that are thought to have originated in Ferrara – Modena C 313 and C 314, and Wolfenbüttel 293.[16] If the compiler of Treviso 30 had connections with Ferrara, he might have obtained Rore's *Si resurrexistis* from the same source. Rore himself can be linked with Treviso through his four-part madrigal *Felice sei Trevigi*, addressed to Treviso and praising 'Giovan Francesco Libertà divino', prior of the Monastery of Santa Margarita and a well-known theologian and preacher.[17] The madrigal may have been commissioned by someone in Treviso to honour Libertà at a particular occasion.[18]

The only unique motet of MS 30 that does not seem to come from the north Italian orbit is Ghiselin Danckerts's *Suscipe Verbum* (no. II/10). Danckerts (ca. 1510–65), a native of the Netherlands, entered the Papal Chapel in 1538 and served there until 1565, when he was 'compelled to retire as a part of a reorganization of the chapel on the grounds that "he has no voice, is exceedingly rich, given to women, useless" '.[19] Danckerts has always been better known as a singer and theorist than as a composer, and most prominently as a judge in the debate between Nicola Vicentino and Vicente Lusitano, which gave rise to his own treatise as well as to Vicentino's. In the article in *The New Grove Dictionary*, Lewis Lockwood lists his extant works as: *Laetamini in domino a 8* in Ulhard, *Concentus 8, 6, 5 et 4 vocum* (RISM 1545[2]), two madrigals on texts by Ariosto in *Primo libro delle Muse* (RISM 1555[27]), four other Ariosto settings attributed to 'Ghiselij' in Brussels, Bibliothèque royale Albert Ier, MS 27731 (Cantus only), and 'several puzzle canons, including 2 in P. Cerone: El Melopeo y maestro (Naples, 1613)'.[20] He also mentions the two motets in Treviso 29 and 30 as 'destroyed during World War II'.

Cipriano de Rore (München, Bayerische Staatsbibliothek, Mus. Ms. B)' (Ph.D. diss., Princeton University, 1979), pp. 226–34.

[16] On the Modena manuscripts, see *Census-Catalogue of Manuscript Sources*, 2, pp. 161–3. In 'Rore's Setting of Petrarch's "Vergine bella": A History of its Composition and Early Transmission', *Journal of Musicology*, 4 (1985–6), 365–409, Mary S. Lewis makes a plausible case that some of the Rore pieces of Wolfenbüttel 293 were copied from an autograph manuscript.

[17] See Bernhard Meier, *Cipriani de Rore Opera Omnia* 5 (Corpus mensurabilis musicae, 14; American Institute of Musicology, 1971), 12–14 and Introduction, p. XI.

[18] The madrigal was first printed in 1565; on stylistic grounds Meier posits that it was composed earlier, perhaps when 'Libertà stopped in Venice in 1543 during Lent' (ibid., p. XI, n. 6).

[19] Lewis Lockwood, 'Danckerts, Ghiselin', *The New Grove Dictionary*, 5 (1980), 220.

[20] Ibid. One of the enigmatic pieces is the famous 'chessboard' on *Ave maris stella*, partially transcribed in Antoine Auda, *La musique et les musiciens de l'Ancien Pays de Liège* (Brussels, 1930), p. 76. In his treatise Danckerts says that it can be sung in more than

Unaccountably missing from this list is *Tua est potentia a 6*, published in Kriesstein, *Selectissimae necnon familiarissimae cantiones* (Augsburg, RISM 1540[7]), no. 2. This is the 'concento a sei voci, con l'inventione del tenore, accomodata sopra li sei gigli dell'Arme di Papa Paulo terzo' that Danckerts mentions in the note to the reader that prefaces his treatise.[21] It was his intention to publish it, together with his two puzzle canons, at the end of that work. In the form in which Kriesstein printed the motet, there is no hint of an enigmatic tenor. It is presented as an ostinato on the text and melody *Da pacem*; see Example 1. The first and third statements are augmented with respect to the ¢ of the other voices. The second statement is sung as written.

Ex. 1

Da-pac-em-Do-mi-ne

It is hard to see how Danckerts could have arranged this tenor 'on the six lilies of the coat of arms of Pope Paul III'. If we turn, however, to Treviso 30, second series, no. 15, we find that the tenor

---

twenty different ways and that it was printed in 1535; see J. de Bruijn, 'Ghisilinus Danckerts, kapelaan-sanger van de Pauselijke kapel van 1538 tot 1565. – Zijn leven, werken en onuitgegeven tractaat', *Tijdschrift der Vereeniging voor nederl. Muziekgeschiedenis*, 16 (1946), 217–52, and 17 (1949), 128–57; see 17, pp. 130–1. In 1549 Melchior Kriesstein brought out a single-page print of it that survives in the Herzog August Bibliothek, Wolfenbüttel; see Wolfgang Schmieder and Gisela Hartwieg, eds., *Musik: Alte Drucke bis etwa 1750, Textband* (Kataloge der Herzog-August-Bibliothek Wolfenbüttel, Die neue Reihe; Frankfurt am Main, 1967), p. 68. For a facsimile (after Cerone, not Bermudo's *Comiença el libro llamado Declaración*, as the caption states), see *Die Musik in Geschichte und Gegenwart*, 1, cols. 1763–4.

The other work is a double canon in the form of a cross with two added voices on the text 'Crucem sanctam subiit' (Cerone, *El Melopeo*, pp. 1138–9). Cerone dates it 1549.

[21] Rome, Biblioteca Vallicelliana, MS R 56, fol. 350. The treatise survives in several redactions. On the title page of one, Danckerts promised to include '16 cantilene a piu voci in diversi idiomi dal medesimo Ghilino [*sic*] nel solo genere Diatonico composte'; on the title page of another, the number is '20'. Unfortunately, none of these works is included in MS R 56, but they are listed on fol. 572v. The 'cantilene della compositione sciolta' (i.e. free, non-canonic compositions) are *La dolce vista*, *Non m'è grave el tormento*, *Fidel qual sempre fui*, *Scarpello si vedrà*, *Perche piangi Alma*, *Clarus es ante alios*, and *Gratias agimus*. The 'cantilene della compositione obligata alli canoni' are: '*Il est bien aise* a 4 voci sopra una, *Tout d'ung accord* a 4 voci sopra due, *Adieu soulas* a 6 voci sopra tre, *Faulte d'argent* a 6 voci sopra quattro, *Petite camusette* a 8 voci sopra cinque, *Pater noster col Ave Maria* a nove voci sopra sei'. These compositions were to be included for the delectation of the public until Danckerts had occasion to publish 'le misse, motetti, hymni, orationi, lamentationi, madrigali, psalmi, cantici et altre cantilene in maggior numero da me nel detto Genere Diatonico solo composte' (fol. 573). Except for the two madrigals *Fedel qual sempre fui* and *Scarpello si vedrà*, printed by Barre in 1555, all these compositions have disappeared without a trace; even the manuscripts of the Cappella Sistina, where Danckerts served for twenty-seven years, preserve no compositions under his name.

(here the *quinta pars*) consists of the stemma of Paul III superimposed on a music staff, with the following canonic directions: 'Vocales docent cantum, quod lilia florent' (see the Inventory below, where D'Alessi's sketch of the coat of arms is reproduced).[22] Danckerts was not one to provide an easy key to the solution. 'The vowels teach the melody, that the lilies may flourish.' The lilies are obvious, but where are the vowels? D'Alessi did not explain the enigma. In fact, the arrangement of the lilies is slightly different from that on official representations of the Pope's stemma,[23] where the three lilies at the top are in a horizontal row. I believe that D'Alessi's sketch is slightly off centre and that the lilies should be superimposed on the staff so that the four central ones fall on the two central spaces, the other two lilies on the lines above and below. If we imagine a tenor clef, the bottom row of lilies yields *re ut re* and the top row *fa sol fa*. If one starts with the *re* lily nearest the clef and sings anti-clockwise, the *Da pacem* melody results. But how does the singer know which lily to start with, and how does he find the necessary pauses and the transposition of the middle statement? Unless D'Alessi's sketch is not complete, the singers could not perform this motet from Treviso 30 without considerable experimentation. Transforming a visual image into a temporal one is not easy. One might reasonably expect that the vertical alignment of the lilies could be translated into consonances; the scoring of the motet quickly dispels this notion.[24] More clues are required than Treviso 30 provides.

Danckerts composed the motet in 1538, the year he entered the Papal Chapel. As a gift for a pope, it required a luxurious presentation. Danckerts had it printed in Naples at his own expense, with a ten-year privilege granted by the city. No copy of this print survives; our only information about it comes from a little book by Adrien de la Fage,[25] who seems to have owned a copy of it, although it is not listed in the catalogue of his library.[26] According to La Fage, the printed version gives the motto in a slightly different form: VOCALES

---

[22] Treviso 30 ascribes the work to M(aitre) Jan, but this is clearly an error.

[23] See, for example, the three illustrations from Sistine manuscripts in Josephus M. Llorens, *Capellae Sixtinae Codices*, Plates 1, 3 and 4.

[24] Allan Atlas, proceeding from the plausible hypothesis that the tenor of Isaac's *Palle, palle* is connected in some manner with the six 'palle' of the Medici stemma, was able to show a number of possible correspondences, but he was unable to explain why the five-note main motif is inverted with respect to the arrangement of the five red *palle* on the coat of arms. See 'Heinrich Isaac's *Palle, palle*: A New Interpretation', *Studien zur italienisch-deutschen Musikgeschichte*, 9 (Analecta Musicologica, 14; Cologne, 1974), 17–25.

[25] *Extraits du Catalogue critique et raisonné d'une petite bibliothèque musicale* [Paris, 1857], pp. 88–9. La Fage transcribes the following statement from the end of the print: 'Impress. Neap. Ianua. 1538 impensis auctoris. Non absque provisionibus cautum est per totum orbem sub excommunicationis poena, aliaque pecuniaria in Urbe Neapoli earumque dominiis, ne quis intra decennium hoc opus imprimat, vendat, vel venale habeat absque auctoris licentia'.

[26] *Catalogue de la Bibliothèque musicale de feu M. J. Adr. de la Fage* (Paris, 1862).

DOCENT, CANTUQUE LILIA FLORENT. It also provides the missing clue, a motto 'Te nunc gens adorat', the vowels of which produce the *soggetto cavato re ut re fa sol fa*, which is indeed the *Da pacem* melody.[27] 'Te' secures *re* as the starting point of the melody. In a way, the motto detracts from the conceit; given the melody, the representation of the coat of arms becomes superfluous, except to fix the correct pitch. Still missing is any indication of the rhythmic disposition of the melody. La Fage's description shows that the print gave the mensuration signs and six breve rests as does Kriesstein.

For La Fage, the transcription of *Tua est potentia* was interesting because it could 'afford acquaintance with the system of composition generally followed before Pierluigi da Palestrina', but he saw no point in 'such useless difficulties that torture the spirit and cause a great waste of time, resulting in nothing but real inanities'.[28] His opinion unwittingly echoes that of Vicentino, Danckerts's archrival, who counselled composers wishing to write enigmatic canons to produce ones that

are pleasing and full of sweetness and harmony and not to write canons on a tower, or a mountain, or a river, or a chessboard [a slap at another composition of Danckerts], or on other things, for those compositions make a lot of noise with many voices and little sweetness of harmony, for in truth such disproportionate fantasies, without the intention of imitating the nature of the words and without pleasing harmony, induce annoyance rather than pleasure in the listener. . . . The goal of music is to satisfy the ear, and not with colours or chess pieces or other fancies that appeal more to the eye than to the ear, but those [compositions] to that purpose that accommodate the words well to the harmony – those will be worthy of being heard. But few will be made in this manner because the steps and leaps are suited neither to the subject nor to the words.[29]

---

[27] La Fage refers to his Pl. VIa for an illustration of the tenor. It is not the coat of arms that he had described earlier but a music staff in which the syllables of the motto replace the lilies of the stemma:

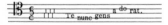

This may be La Fage's own resolution; it is hard to imagine that Danckerts would have spelled out his enigma so clearly. As I had surmised, the clef is a tenor clef, which permits the stemma to be centred on the staff and produce the right pitches. The original surely had a B♭ in the signature.

[28] *Extraits du Catalogue*, p. 89. His transcription is found on pp. 14–19 of the musical supplement.

[29] '. . . il Compositore di tal fantasie, dè cercare di fare Canoni, & altre fughe, che siano gratiate, & piene di dolcezza, et d'armonia, et quello non dè far un Canon sopra una Torre, ò sopra un Monte, ò sopra un fiume, ò sopra i scacchi da giocare, ò sopra altre cose, & che quelle compositioni faccino un gran rumore, à molte voci, con poca dolcezza d'armonia, che per dir il vero queste tal fantasie sproportionate, & senza proposito de imitar la natura delle parole, & senza grata Armonia, induce l'oditore più presto à fastidio che à diletto . . .; il fine della Musica è di satisfare à gl'orecchi, & non con i colori, ò scachi, ò d'altre fantasie che paiono più belle à gl'occhi, che à gl'orecchi,

This advice was ignored by Costanzo Porta, who used the conceit of an enigmatic tenor based on a coat of arms in his thirteen-voice *Missa ducalis*, composed for Duke Cosimo de' Medici between 1565 and 1569. On the splendidly illustrated opening folio of the manuscript, the Medici stemma is set on a five-line staff with an alto clef and a flat. Wound around a large wreath surrounding the stemma is a banderole with the words PROTEGE COSMUM DUCEM. A banderole twisted around a smaller wreath forming part of the coat of arms has PRINCIPEMQUE FRANCISCUM. The *palle* are placed on the staff so that they yield the notes *f a c' d' c' a*. Since the text has seven syllables, *f* must be repeated at the end. Unlike Danckerts, Porta is eager to explain his enigma. Beneath the illumination is an eight-line Latin poem explaining how to find the pitches and beneath that a chart showing the necessary pauses, mensurations and starting pitch for each entry of the ostinato. And just in case any doubt remained, on the next three pages the 'Resolutio subiecti' is spelled out with all desirable clarity.[30]

Physical description

Manuscripts have strange fates. It was the fate of Treviso 29 and 30 to have been destroyed before the use of microfilm became common.[31] But a hundred years had passed since the invention of photography, and it happens that two motets, one in each manuscript, have survived in photographs. They are herewith presented as Plates 1–3 and 5–9.[32] Shortly after the war, J. de Bruijn published an article on Danckerts. [33] He listed no concordances for the two Danckerts works

---

ma quelle che in tal proposito saranno bene accompagnate dall'armonia insieme con le parole; quelle saranno degne d'esser udite, ma poche ci saranno di tal maniera fatte, perche i gradi & i salti non possono servire, ne à tal suggetto, ne alle parole'; *L'antica musica ridotta alla moderna prattica* (Rome, 1555) (facs. ed. by Edward E. Lowinsky, *Documenta Musicologica*, 17; Kassel, 1959), fol. 93v.

[30] The presentation copy is MS Palat. 6 of the Biblioteca Medicea Laurenziana in Florence. A modern edition of the Mass appears in vol. 10 of the *Opera omnia*, ed. Siro Cisilino and Giovanni Luisetto (Padua, 1964). On the dating of the Mass, see Lilian P. Pruett, 'Porta, Costanzo', *The New Grove Dictionary*, 15 (1980), 130. For the description of the canon I used the notes and microfilm of ¨dward Lowinsky.

[31] MS Treviso 3, however, was microfilmed by Laurence Feininger before the war, with the result that not only the film but two complete transcriptions of the manuscript exist, one by Laurence Feininger in a volume of his transcriptions now in the Pontificio Istituto di Musica Sacra in Rome, the other by Don Siro Cisilino in the Biblioteca Capitolare in Treviso. Cisilino remarks, in his prefatory note, that had this manuscript not been saved, we would know hardly anything of the work of Nicolò Olivetto, and no hymns of Giovanni Nasco would have survived.

[32] The ink shows through from the other side of the page, which makes some notes difficult to read. The seminimim that appears to begin the *Quinta pars* of *Tu es vas electionis* (Plate 2b) actually belongs to the motet on the reverse.

[33] See n. 20.

in Treviso 29 and 30, but it was obvious that he had scored them. The article was derived from his thesis, written under the direction of Mgr Raffaele Casimiri and presented in May 1942 to the Pontificio Istituto di Musica Sacra in Rome. Only one of the motets was included in transcription, the piece from Treviso 29. A request to Father de Bruijn for permission to include the transcription in the present study brought forth an entirely unexpected response: enclosed with his letter were fifteen pages of photographs of the two motets.[34] Thanks to Father de Bruijn's generosity, it has been possible to restore to music history not only an illustration of the lost manuscripts but also part of Ghiselin Danckerts's small legacy.

The photographs of the Danckerts motet from MS 29 (see Plates 1–3) allow us to amplify the physical description of the manuscript given by D'Alessi. Surprisingly, the part-books are in an upright, not the usual oblong, format. We still do not know the size of the page, but I would venture a guess that it was somewhat larger than the ordinary size of printed part-books (the photographs measure 225 × 170 mm, but may not include all of the margins),[35] perhaps the size of Willaert's *Musica nova*, measuring 244 × 170 mm, which Gardano printed in upright quarto.[36] Indeed, the *Musica nova*, in addition to being the source for ten motets (nos. 32, 41, 57, 59, II/35–40), may have been the model for Treviso 29; the format is similar, and both have nine staves per page. The music of MS 29 is copied in a neat but not professional hand, which may also be responsible for the modest calligraphic initials. Even the text seems modelled on the roman font used by Gardano in the *Musica nova* of 1559 and later publications (see Plate 4).

Treviso 30 (see Plates 5–9) seems to be a twin of Treviso 29 in its format, but not in its handwriting. At first glance, one is struck by the similarity of the music and text in both manuscripts. Upon closer examination, the differences become apparent: the clefs and custodes differ slightly; ascenders in MS 30 (l, b, h – but not d) have serifs sharply bent back to the left, those in MS 29 have no serifs; MS 30 does not use the long 's' at the end of words. And yet, the similarities in the shapes of individual letters – particularly m, n, e, a, r, t – the repetition signs, and the closing flourish at the end of each *pars* are unmistakable. It is quite possible that the two manuscripts were

---

[34] Letter of 16 July 1978. The goddess Fortuna must have smiled on the postal service, because the envelope arrived completely open on one side. Nothing was missing. Father de Bruijn informed me that he had prepared an English edition of his thesis, but plans for publication came to naught.

[35] Gardane's oblong quartos vary from 142 × 204 to 159 × 216 mm; Lewis, 'Antonio Gardane', p. 41.

[36] Ibid., p. 46; the measurements are of the British Library copy. Lewis remarks that Gardane reserved this unusual format for 'a few works of special importance'. The Ferrarese part-books Modena C 313 and C 314 are also in this format, but much larger in size; they measure 355 × 245 mm and have ten staves per page; see *Census-Catalogue*, pp. 161–2.

copied by the same person, but that a period of several years intervened. Such changes in style are more likely in the case of unprofessional copyists than in the scriptoria of institutions such as the Sistine Chapel, where a conscious attempt seems to have been made to use one clearly established style. The handwriting does not match those found in the Treviso choirbooks, as far as I can determine.[37]

Treviso 29 bore the initials and coat of arms of Varisco; apparently MS 30 had no distinguishing marks. While MS 29 does not appear in the inventory of the cathedral's music manuscripts drawn up by Francesco Veretoni between 1574 and 1595,[38] there is an entry, under 'Libri vechi di chiesa', that D'Alessi believed referred to MS 30: 'Sei libri in quarto. Da Motetti coverti simili' (i.e. 'de Carton et bergamina', cardboard and vellum). He identified this entry with the 'sei libri di mottetti, altra volta scritti da messer pre Francisco Santa Croce Maestro de capella' that were rebound in 1574 because they were 'tutti ro[v]inati'.[39] Santacroce was choirmaster at Treviso from 1520 to 1528 and again from 1537 to 1551. His death date is not known; Denis Arnold suggests that he 'perhaps may be identified with a canon of Loreto Cathedral who died in 1556'.[40] These six books of motets were probably written during his tenure as choirmaster, but even 1551 seems too early a date for the contents of MS 30, especially the works by Nasco, who arrived in Treviso six months after Santacroce's departure, Alberti (born ca. 1535) and Metallo, and the Willaert motet that was probably taken from *Musica nova* (no. 19). It seems likely, therefore, that MS 30 belonged to Varisco as well as MS 29 and that it dates from a few years earlier than the 1575 *terminus ante quem non* that I have posited for MS 29.

---

[37] I have examined films of MSS 7, 8, 9, 10, 14 and 24, and photographs from MSS 11 and 13 in D'Alessi, *La Cappella musicale*, Figs. 7 and 10.

[38] The title on the outside cover had '1574. 1. luio. Registro de li libri lasciati al R.do Capitolo di Treviso per il quondam messer liberal Sugana. Fu sepelito adì 6 febraro 1574', but the catalogue included all the music manuscripts, not just those of Sugana. At the end, before the last group of printed books, there was the heading '1595. primo zenaro'. For a transcription of the catalogue, see D'Alessi, *La Cappella musicale*, pp. 180–2.

[39] Ibid., pp. 178–9 and n. 4.

[40] 'Santa Croce, Francesco', *The New Grove Dictionary*, 16 (1980), 475.

5

The Newly Recovered Motets

Ghiselin Danckerts, Tu es vas electionis a 5

The recovery of two lost pieces by Ghiselin Danckerts doubles his surviving output as a motet composer. De Bruijn, who knew the lost works, praised Danckerts's eight-voice *Laetamini in Domino*, published by Ulhard in 1545, as 'a real jewel',[1] but he was puzzled by *Tu es vas electionis* from Treviso 29. He felt that the melodic style and text setting were deficient and did not agree with the style of Danckerts's other motets, so much so that he raised the question whether *Tu es vas* might not be the work of another composer.[2] I am fortunate to be able to vindicate de Bruijn's intuition; *Tu es vas electionis* is a contrafactum of Dominicus Phinot's *Tua est potentia*, published in the same print from which Varisco copied seven motets by Phinot, the *Liber primus mutetarum quinque vocum* (Gardane, 1552), providing two of them with contrafactum texts. Survival of the photographs not only allows us to confirm that Gardane's print is indeed Varisco's source, but affords a glimpse into the workshop of this wholesale manufacturer of 'new' motets.

Phinot's motet is a setting of the responsory *Tua es potentia*. The opening phrase of the text is one syllable longer in the contrafactum version, but both phrases fit the music well with only a few changes in rhythm (Example 2). The only poor accentuation is the same in both motets: the melisma on a weak syllable in the *quinta pars* in bars 5–6. The third phrase of text in *Tu es vas electionis* is twice as long as that in *Tua est potentia*, but since Phinot habitually sets a phrase of text at least twice, there are enough notes to accommodate the longer text

---

[1] De Bruijn, 'Ghisilinus Danckerts', p. 135.

[2] 'Het stuk is niet gelukkig en maakt vele grillige rhythmen en moeilijk zingbare sprongen; vele woorden worden verwrongen en stuntelig gedeclameerd, een onromeinse tekstzegging, die strijdt met wat we aan kunde in dit opzicht in andere motetten van Danckerts zien' ('The work is infelicitous and has many irregular rhythms and awkward leaps; many words are distorted and incorrectly declaimed; the non-humanistic text setting conflicts with what we see in this regard in Danckerts's other motets'); ibid., p. 137.

Ex. 2

1) Treviso 29:

Ex. 3

of the contrafactum. The greatest rhythmic changes come in the B section of the responsory. Here Varisco has altered the rhythm so skilfully that one might be tempted to consider the contrafactum text the original (Example 3).

Ex. 4

Varisco's revisions do not merely consist of changed rhythms. When he reached the *secunda pars*, the verse of the responsory, he was faced with a problem. In *Tua est potentia*, the text runs as follows: 'Creator omnium Deus terribilis et fortis, iustus et misericors'. In *Tu es vas* the text is seven syllables shorter: 'Intercede pro nobis ad Deum qui te elegit'. Instead of stretching the text out over the eleven and a half bars that Phinot assigned to 'iustus et misericors', Varisco simply cut them out, as if with a scalpel (see Example 4; bars 10–11 are followed directly by bar 22₃, with no alterations at the joining point). With the omission of a fractional bar, Varisco's version would have

Ex. 4 continued

ended in the middle of a bar, a compositional *faux pas*.[3] Instead of recomposing the succeeding B section to incorporate or delete half a bar, Varisco re-used the B section of the *prima pars*, beginning on the downbeat of bar 35. The scar from the graft can still be seen in the superius at bar 12 (see Plate 1a, end of staff 7). The breve G was originally followed by a semibreve A and a semibreve pause, which is the ending of the 'a' section of the responsory. The A was subsequently erased (it caused parallel 13ths with the bass) but not replaced by a pause.

Proof that Gardane's Phinot book rather than the Lyons print of 1547 was the source of Varisco's contrafactum may be found in the superius on the second staff (see Plate 1a). A semibreve F has been crowded in and a semibreve rest scratched out at the end of the phrase. The reason for the change lies in Gardane's omission of the dotted minim B♭ and semiminim A in bar 11_{2-3} (see Example 2). The mistake was caught only after the motet had been copied, but the wrong correction was made (see Example 2, note 1); it causes a dissonance on the last beat of bar 11 and misplaces the characteristic cadential suspension.

In the absence of further examples from Varisco's motet workshop, it is a moot point whether he generally proceeded as in *Tua est potentia/Tu es vas*. But two further observations can be made. Varisco usually chose a contrafactum text with a form, but not necessarily liturgical category, similar to the original text; an *oratio*, for example, may replace an antiphon. With responsories he took greater freedom. Comes's *Cum iocunditate* (II/5) was evidently recast into a two-part motet based on two antiphons (no. 53) – unless Varisco used a responsory text that I have not discovered. Rore's psalm motet *In Domino confido* and Gombert's *Caeciliam cantate* were changed to responsories (nos. 88 and 113). Whether Varisco altered the music to reflect the normal aBcB setting of responsory texts we do not know, but his revision of Phinot's *Tua est potentia* shows that he was capable of more than minor changes, when the text of the contrafactum demanded it.

---

[3] On this point see Pietro Aaron, *Toscanello in musica* (Venice, 1529), Book I, ch. 39, 'Come i cantori hanno a numerare i canti', fol. F2v: '. . . in ciascun canto conviene che si ritruovi modo, tempo, et prolatione, come nel principio fu detto: essendo un canto di modo maggior perfetto: è necessario che in tutto il suo discorso gli sia la quantità di detto modo: la quale è il numero di tre longhe: similmente nel modo minore perfetto di tre brevi: nel tempo perfetto di tre semibrevi: et ne la prolation perfetta di tre minime. Per la qual cosa non si trovando la quantità predetta: sarà da noi attribuito grandissimo errore a quegli che 'l contrario usano' ('Every composition must consist of mode, *tempus* and prolation, as was said in the beginning. If a composition is in the major perfect mode, it must be measured throughout in the quantity of that mode, i.e. in units of three longs; similarly, in the minor perfect mode in units of three breves, and in perfect time in three semibreves, and in perfect prolation in three minims. Therefore if the stated quantity is not present, we impute a grave error to those who do not observe this').

How Varisco went about choosing a contrafactum text is a question to which some answers can be suggested. Foremost among his concerns was the rhythm of the opening phrase. In many of the contrafacta the first few notes are rhythmically identical with the originals. In other cases the choice of text seems to have been prompted by melodic considerations. Phinot's *Tanto tempore*, which opens with a descending fifth, was reset to the text 'Descendit Spiritus Sanctus' (no. 4). Simple assonance may be another reason: *Agatha laetissime/Auribus percipe* (no. 13), *Tu es vas electionis/Tua est potentia* (no. 9). In two examples, the Gregorian melody associated with the contrafactum text closely resembles the opening of the motets chosen as models. Portinaro's *Dum esset summus Pontifex* (no. 115) is a contrafactum of his *Da pacem Domine*; the first six pitches of the respective Gregorian melodies are very similar. Rore's psalm motet *Usquequo Domine* begins with a motif close to the responsory melody of *Regnum mundi*, the contrafactum text chosen by Varisco (no. 123), who also placed the second and third notes in ligature, matching the chant (Example 5). Both melodies are in the fifth mode, and the F-A-C opening recalls the beginning of the fifth psalm tone.

Ex. 5

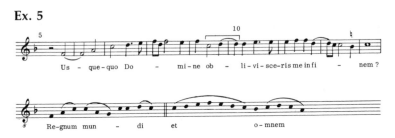

This is a second psalm motet by Rore that was turned into a responsory; since psalms had no place in the liturgical arrangement of Treviso 29, and since motets set in two *partes* are often on responsory texts, this was a logical choice. However, for some of Rore's psalm motets consisting of more than one *pars*, Varisco selected only the *prima pars* and gave it an antiphon text.

Ghiselin Danckerts, Suscipe Verbum a 6

Danckerts's *Suscipe Verbum* from MS 30, published here for the first time (see Musical Appendix, no. 1), is a setting of the responsory for Marian feasts (*Proc. Mon.* 245). It does not draw on the Gregorian melody. The *quinta pars* sings a *cantus firmus* on the text and melody of the well-known antiphon *Ave Maria* (L.U. 1679), transposed up a fourth, to which is added the *repetenda* of the responsory at bar 52 in both *partes*. Since MS 30 was missing the *sexta pars* part-book before 1944, a voice is lacking. After vain attempts to find the canonic leader of the *cantus firmus*, labelled 'Resolutio' (see Plate 7),[4] I realized that the missing voice is not canonic. It is a second bass. Danckerts followed the not uncommon custom of exchanging voices at the second B section in a responsory setting. Fortunately, it was the basses that he exchanged in *Suscipe Verbum*, so the second half of each *pars*, from bar 53 on, can be reconstructed in its entirety. Only the first fifty-two bars of each *pars* are now lacking. I offer a reconstruction of the missing voice, not without trepidation. As may be seen in the B section, where all six parts are extant, Danckerts was skilled in arranging the voices in imitative counterpoint with few pauses. Finding the imitative entries in the missing voice was not too difficult, but I have probably left more spaces between the phrases than Danckerts did. And I am not satisfied with two passages (*1.p.*, bars 31–4 and 49–52).

Four motets by Trevisan choirmasters

Through the discovery of the contrafacta, the number of unica in Treviso 29 has dropped from sixty-five works to five. But thanks once more to the foresight of Giovanni D'Alessi, two of these five works survive in transcriptions made by him long before the war; they are housed with his papers in the Biblioteca Capitolare. Two unica from MS 30 were among them as well.[5] The newly recovered motets are two works by Giovanni Nasco, *Inviolata, integra et casta es* from MS 29 (no. II/1) and the *prima pars* of *Memor esto* from MS 30 (no. II/5); a work of Francesco Santacroce, *Domine Deus omnipotens* (MS 30, no. 9); and Pietro Antonio Spalenza's *Deus alma spes* (MS 29, no. 71). These four works are presented in the Appendix.

Nasco, Santacroce and Spalenza were all *maestri di cappella* at Treviso Cathedral. In the appendix to his book, D'Alessi published two works by Santacroce, a prayer for Venice and a double-choir psalm, and one by Nasco, a harmonically colourful and expressive motet for four voices, *Tristis est anima mea*.

Pietro Antonio Spalenza, *maestro di cappella* at Treviso Cathedral from 1573 until some time in 1577,[6] was not a prolific composer. He published one book of madrigals in 1574,[7] and a *falsobordone* is found

---

[4] The cantus firmus may originally have been written in an enigmatic manner, as was the cantus firmus of Danckerts's *Tua est potentia* (see above, pp. 40–42). It is precisely the same in both *partes*.

[5] I wish to extend my warmest thanks to Mgr Angelo Campagner, Director of the Biblioteca Capitolare, for helping me search for transcriptions of lost works during my visit in 1981. He took two of the transcriptions on the spot to the episcopal offices to be photocopied; the remaining two were discovered at the last minute, and he was kind enough to send photocopies of them to me in Chicago.

[6] D'Alessi, *La Cappella musicale*, pp. 123–6.

[7] *Il Primo Libro di Madrigali a quattro voci, di Pietr' Antonio Spalenza, bresciano, maestro di*

in MS Q 12 of the Civico Museo Bibliografico Musicale in Bologna.[8] Seven of his works were preserved in manuscripts at Treviso; only one, the hymn *Ad preces nostras* in MS 13, survived the war.[9] Thus Spalenza's *Deus alma spes* from MS 29 (see Musical Appendix, no. 2) is his only extant motet. It is a setting of the antiphon to the Magnificat at First Vespers on the Feast of SS Theonistus, Tabra and Tabrata (22 November), local saints whose bodies lie in the Duomo of Treviso (see above, p. 9). The Quintus carries an ostinato on the text 'Sancti Theoniste Tabra et Tabrata orate pro nobis', sung four times in identical form. Spalenza's motet is an attractive, sonorous work in Mixolydian that tends towards the major, with numerous F sharps indicated. The beginning and ending of the ostinato call for cadences on the tonic, and they appear elsewhere as well, producing a strong harmonic feeling in a work that is contrapuntally worked out, but not in the manner of northern composers; Spalenza, like some of his Italian colleagues, feels free to use more than one theme for a phrase of text (see in particular the opening), and his imitations often do not extend beyond two or three notes. His small output is probably due to an early death rather than to lack of talent.

Francesco Santacroce, also called Patavino, directed the choir at the cathedral from 1520 to 1528 and again from 1537 to 1551.[10] Aside from ten psalms for double choir in Treviso 11, 22 and 24, he is the author of five motets, two of which (including Musical Appendix, no. 3) survive only in transcriptions.[11] Two others are lost and one is still extant in Treviso 7. *Domine Deus omnipotens*, from Treviso 30, is a five-voice setting in pervading imitation of the prayer said at Prime after the Confession and Absolution (L.U. 232). Santacroce obviously admired the polyphonic style of the Netherlanders, and he made a creditable effort to imitate it. After a typical beginning, however, his Italian roots begin to show. Melodic and rhythmic invention are subordinated to harmonic conception. Absent are the lengthy imitative passages of his northern confrères; Santacroce's motifs are usually limited to three or four notes. In this motet in transposed Dorian Santacroce moves first to the related key area of untransposed

---

capella del domo di Treviso, novamente composti et dati in luce. Libro Primo. In Venetia appresso li figliuoli di Antonio Gardano. 1574 (RISM 1574⁹).

[8] See Gaetano Gaspari, *Catalogo della Biblioteca del Liceo Musicale di Bologna*, 4 (Bologna, 1905), 235, and Lewis Lockwood, *The Counter-Reformation and the Masses of Vincenzo Ruffo* (Studi di Musica Veneta, 2; Vienna, 1970), p. 247.

[9] The list of works is given in D'Alessi, *La Cappella musicale*, p. 125. The statement in *The New Grove Dictionary*, 17, 'Spalenza', p. 815, that 'a number of sacred works for four to twelve voices and *falsi bordoni* for four voices survive in manuscript' was true only until April 1944.

[10] D'Alessi, *La Cappella musicale*, pp. 67–71 and 84–9.

[11] The one motet by Santacroce that appears in a modern edition is missing from the work list given by Denis Arnold in his article on the composer in *The New Grove Dictionary*, 16, p. 475. It is *Praecamur te Pater* from Treviso 4, published by D'Alessi as no. 1 in the musical appendix to his book.

Dorian, but the whole middle section revolves around B♭, requiring many E♭s, which sometimes cause cross-relations (see bars 45–6 and 56). In his prayer for Venice, published by D'Alessi, and in his double-choir psalms, Santacroce remains closer to his native roots in a melismatically animated homophonic style.

Among the *maestri di cappella* at the Duomo of Treviso in the sixteenth century, nearly all of whom were composers, Giovanni Nasco was the most illustrious. Sixty-five of his compositions were entered into the cathedral's choirbooks after his arrival in Treviso towards the end of 1551.[12] Twenty-three survived the bombardment. D'Alessi, who must have transcribed a number of Nasco's works, found evidence of haste in some – we recall that Nasco complained that the feast days kept him very busy (see above, p. 13) – but in general classified him among the good polyphonists of the century. He singled out for praise a few works in particular, including *Inviolata, integra et casta* from MS 29,[13] published below as no. 4. The motet, loosely based on the sequence melody (L.U. 1861), was written for five high voices with two parts in G clefs, one soprano, one mezzo-soprano and one alto clef, and must have been sung by choirboys on feasts of the Virgin.[14] Nasco's long years in Italy are manifest in his harmonically oriented counterpoint and his concern for good declamation. The high pitch, the narrow range of two octaves, the uncommon modal disposition, in which the soprano, alto and bass are in the authentic range, the tenor and quintus in the plagal, and the nearly continuous full texture give this motet an unusual sound.[15] One wonders if Nasco did not see in his mind's eye a representation of the Queen of Heaven surrounded by singing cherubs and angels. The vocal ranges of angels have not yet been determined, but it seems unlikely that they sang bass.[16]

The six-part motet *Memor esto* from MS 30, set to verses 49–50 of Psalm 118, is likewise written for high voices (see Musical Appendix, no. 5). Although D'Alessi transcribed only the *prima pars*, it is complete; in this case the missing *sexta pars* part-book contained the resolution of the canonic *quinta pars*, so the part can be reconstructed

---

[12] D'Alessi, *La Cappella musicale*, ch. IX, pp. 105–17.

[13] For his discussion, see ibid., p. 116.

[14] It may have been a custom at Treviso as well as elsewhere to give the *Inviolata* to choirboys to sing; Basiron and Ghiselin also composed settings with a high soprano, and anonymous settings in a high range of transmitted in Uppsala, Universitetsbiblioteket, Vok mus i hs 76c, fol. 97v, and Petrucci, *Motetti L. IV*, no. 35.

[15] A few irregular dissonances should be noted: the simultaneous fifth and sixth above the bass in bar 3, the relatively accented fourth in bar 38 and *secunda pars*, bar 23, the cross-relation that gives the effect of a chromatic semitone in bar 47, the missing bass note in *secunda pars*, bar 29. None of these seems to result from an error in copying.

[16] David Fallows kindly reminded me that my view of the angelic spectrum is too narrow: 'certainly the archangels were men, Michael and Gabriel; so was Lucifer, though one could conceivably argue that his voice broke when he fell from grace; and throughout the Bible angels are consistently referred to as men'.

without difficulty. The cantus firmus is an ostinato on the text 'Servus tuus ego sum, Domine ne despicias'. Remarkable are the contrasts in colour between the two statements of 'Be mindful of your word', the first in the minor, the second in the major. Many of the E♭s are written in; one cautionary natural occurs when a flat might normally be sung by *musica ficta* (see bar 13). The B♮ in the bass of bar 4 is puzzling; it certainly cannot stand. *Memor esto* might have been composed as a gentle reminder of an unkept promise because it uses only the first two or three verses of the fourth section of Psalm 118 (the *secunda pars* is missing and we cannot tell how far the text went, but it is unlikely that it was much longer than the *prima pars*, which consists of one psalm verse). The manifold repetition of the words 'in which you have given me hope' surely must have brought the point home.

Epilogue

The unmasking of sixty unica as contrafacta, the recovery of five lost compositions, and the reappearance of photographs of one motet from each manuscript have allowed the reconstruction of Treviso 29 and 30 in form, if only partly in substance. Yet even this shadowy restoration of Pietro Varisco's manuscript and its companion volume Treviso 30 has allowed us to determine what the manuscripts contained, when they were copied and what they looked like. In the case of MS 29, it has even been possible to discover the sources and to learn how one sixteenth-century musician went about creating contrafacta so that music he liked could be sung in his church on all high feast days. Above all, it has been possible to lay to rest the myth of a manuscript full of compositions of great masters not found in any other source. The disastrous fire of 1944 that destroyed so many of the capitular library's treasures consumed part of the substance but not the spirit of the musical tradition at the Duomo of Treviso. That spirit lived on in Giovanni D'Alessi, and through his research and publications it continues to illuminate our understanding of musical life at Treviso Cathedral in the late sixteenth century.

Plate 1. Gislinus, *Tu es vas electionis*, Cantus and Altus (Treviso 29, no. 9)

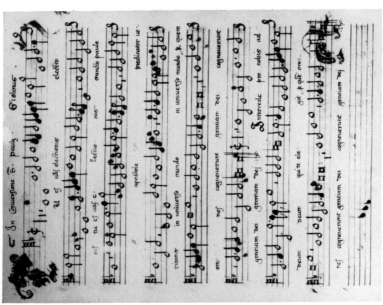

Plate 2.   Gislinus, *Tu es vas electionis*, Tenor and Quintus (Treviso 29, no. 9)

Plate 3. Gislinus, *Tu es vas electionis*, Bassus (Treviso, 29, no. 9)

Plate 4. Adrian Willaert, *Musica nova* (Venice: A. Gardano, 1559), Tenor, p. 21

Plate 5. Ghislinus Danckerts, *Suscipe Verbum*, Cantus (Treviso 30, 2nd series, no. 10)

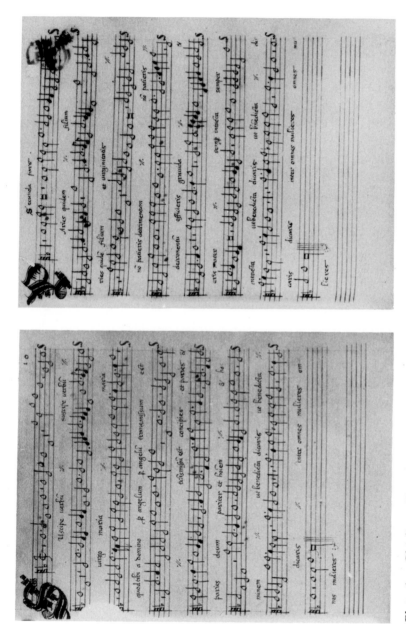

Plate 6.   Ghislinus Danckerts, *Suscipe Verbum*, Altus (Treviso 30, 2nd series, no. 10)

Plate 7. Ghislinus Danckerts, *Suscipe Verbum*, Quintus (Treviso 30, 2nd series, no. 10)

Plate 8.   Ghislinus Danckerts, *Suscipe Verbum*, Tenor (Treviso 30, 2nd series, no. 10)

Plate 9.   Ghislinus Danckerts, *Suscipe Verbum*, Bassus (Treviso 30, 2nd series, no. 10)

Inventory

Sources

A. Manuscripts

Bologna Q 19	Bologna, Civico Museo Bibliografico Musicale, MS Q 19
Bologna SP 31	Bologna, Archivio Musicale della Fabbriceria di San Petronio, MS A. XXXI
Bologna SP 39	Bologna, Archivio Musicale della Fabbriceria di San Petronio, MS A. XXXIX
C.S. 13	Vatican City, Biblioteca Apostolica Vaticana, MS Cappella Sistina 13
C.S. 38	Vatican City, Biblioteca Apostolica Vaticana, MS Cappella Sistina 38
C.S. 46	Vatican City, Biblioteca Apostolica Vaticana, MS Cappella Sistina 46
Edinburgh 64	Edinburgh, University Library, MS 64 (*olim* Db.I.7)
Florence 11	Florence, Duomo, Archivio Musicale dell'Opera di Santa Maria del Fiore, MS 11
Lucca 775	Lucca, Biblioteca Statale, MS 775
Modena C 313	Modena, Biblioteca Estense e Universitaria, MS C. 313
Modena C 314	Modena, Biblioteca Estense e Universitaria, MS C. 314
Munich B	Munich, Bayerische Staatsbibliothek, Mus. Ms. B
Munich 45	Munich, Bayerische Staatsbibliothek, Mus. Ms. 45
Piacenza	Piacenza, Archivio del Duomo, MS s.s. marked Quintus

Regensburg AR 893	Regensburg, Bischöfliche Zentralbibliothek, MS A.R. 893
Toledo 17	Toledo, Biblioteca Capitular, MS 17
Treviso	Treviso, Biblioteca Capitolare del Duomo
Vallicelliana	Rome, Biblioteca Vallicelliana, MS S^I 35–40
Wolfenbüttel 293	Wolfenbüttel, Herzog August Bibliothek, MS Guelf 293

B. Printed Anthologies

Antico 1521[5]	Motetti libro quarto
Gardane 1539[3]	Primus liber cum sex vocibus. Mottetti del frutto a sei voci
Gardane 1542[10]	Adriani Willaert . . . musicorum sex vocum, que vulgo motecta dicuntur . . . liber primus
Gardane 1544[6]	Cipriani musici eccelentissimi cum quibusdam aliis doctis authoribus motectorum . . . liber primus quinque vocum
Gardane 1549[6]	Musica quinque vocum que materna lingua moteta vocantur ab optimis et varijs authoribus elaborata paribus vocibus decantanda
Gardane 1549[8]	Il terzo libro di motetti a cinque voci di Cipriano de Rore et de altri eccellentissimi musici novamente ristampato con una buona gionta de motetti novi
Gardane 1553[17]	Iachet musici suavissimi celeberrimique musices . . . motecta quinque vocum
Kriesstein 1540[7]	Selectissimae necnon familiarissimae cantiones
Kriesstein 1545[3]	Cantiones septem, sex et quinque vocum
Moderne 1532[9]	Secundus liber cum quinque vocibus
Moderne 1538[2]	Tertius liber mottetorum ad quinque et sex voces
Moderne 1542[5]	Quintus liber mottetorum ad quinque et sex et septem vocum
Montanus & Neuber 1554[10]	Evangelia dominicorum et festorum dierum . . . Tomi primi
Montanus & Neuber 1555[11]	Tertius tomus Evangeliorum, quatuor, quinque, sex et plurium vocum

Montanus & Neuber [1556][9]	Sextus tomus Evangeliorum, et piarum sententiarum. Quatuor, sex, et octo vocum
Phalèse 1553[11]	Liber quartus cantionum sacrarum (vulgo moteta vocant) quinque et sex vocum
Rhau 1545[5]	Officiorum (ut vocant) de Nativitate, Circumcisione, Epiphania Domini, & Purificatione &c. Tomus primus
Schoeffer 1539[8]	Cantiones quinque vocum selectissimae . . . Mutetarum liber primus
Scotto 1541[3]	Nicolai Gomberti musici excellentissimi Pentaphthongos harmonia, que quinque vocum Motetta vulgo nominantur
Susato 1546[7]	Liber secundus sacrarum cantionum, quinque vocum vulgo moteta vocant
Susato 1557[3]	Liber duodecimus ecclesiasticarum cantionum quinque vocum vulgo moteta vocant

C. Prints of single authors

Animuccia 1552	Il primo libro dei motetti a cinque voci (Rome: Valerio and Aloisio Dorico, 1552)
Comes 1547	El Conte. Bartholomei Comitis Gallici eccellentissimi musici motetta quinque vocibus suavissime sonantia (Venice: A. Gardane, 1547)
Continus 1560/1	Ioannis Contini . . . modulationum quinque vocum liber primus (Venice: G. Scotto, 1560)
Continus 1560/2	Ioannis Contini . . . modulationum quinque vocum liber secundus (Venice: G. Scotto, 1560)
Continus 1560/3	Ioannis Contini . . . modulationum sex vocum liber primus (Venice: G. Scotto, 1560)
Corvus 1555	Corvi Novocomensis mutettorum quinque vocum liber primus (Venice: A. Gardane, 1555)
Garulli 1562	Modulationum quinque vocum . . . liber primus (Venice: G. Scotto, 1562)
Gombert 1541	Nicolai Gomberti musici solertissimi motectorum quinque vocum . . . liber secundus (Venice: G. Scotto, 1541)

Gombert 1550	Nicolai Gomberti musici solertissimi motectorum quinque vocum . . . liber secundus (Venice: G. Scotto, 1550)
Gombert 1552	Nicolai Gomberti musici excellentissimi cum quinque vocibus liber secundus (Venice: A. Gardane, 1552)
Jachet 1540	Primo libro di mottetti di Iachet a cinque voci (Venice: A. Gardane, 1540)
Jachet 1557	Missa ad imitationem moduli, Surge Petre Auctore Jacquet cum sex vocibus (Paris: LeRoy & Ballard, 1557)
Lasso 1562	Orlandi Lassi sacrae cantiones (vulgo motecta appellatae) quinque vocum . . . liber primus (Venice: A. Gardano, 1562)
Lupi 1542	Jo. Lupi . . . musice cantiones (que vulgo motetta nuncupantur) (Paris: Attaingnant and Jullet, 1542)
Palestrina 1572	Johannis Petraloysii Praenestini motettorum quae partim quinis, partim senis, partim octonis vocibus concinantur. Liber secundus (Venice: G. Scotto, 1572)
Palestrina 1575	Johannis Petraloysii Praenestini motettorum quae partim quinis, partim senis, partim octonis vocibus concinantur. Liber tertius (Venice: Heirs of G. Scotto, 1575)
Phinot 1552	Liber primus mutetarum quinque vocum, Dominico Phinot autore (Venice: A. Gardane, 1552)
Portinaro 1548	Primi frutti di Francesco Portinaro Padoano de motetti a cinque voci . . . libro primo (Venice: A. Gardano, 1548)
Portinaro 1568	Di Francesco Portinaro il secondo libro de motteti a sei sette et otto voci (Venice: A. Gardano, 1568)
Rore 1545	Cypriani Rore musici excellentissimi motetta . . . quinque vocum (Venice: A. Gardane, 1545)
Ruffo 1555	Motetti a sei voci composti da Vincentio Ruffo (Venice: G. Scotto, 1555)
Willaert 1539 or 1550	Famosissimi Adriani Willaert . . . Musica quinque vocum . . . liber primus (Venice: G. Scotto, 1539 and 1550)

Willaert 1559	*Musica nova di Adriano Willaert* (Venice: A. Gardano, 1559)
Zarlino 1549	*Josephi Zarlini musici quinque vocum moduli, motecta vulgo nuncupata . . . liber primus* (Venice: A. Gardane, 1549)
Zarlino 1566	*Josephi Zarlini Clodiensis musici celeberrimi . . . modulationes sex vocum* (Venice: F. Rampazetto, 1566)

Abbreviations

A.H.	*Analecta Hymnica*, ed. G. M. Dreves and C. Blume, 55 vols. (Leipzig, 1886–1922)
Ant. Mon.	*Antiphonale Monasticum pro diurnis horis . . . ordinis Sancti Benedicti* (Paris, Tournai, Rome, 1934)
Ant. Rom.	*Antiphonale Sacrosanctae Romanae Ecclesiae* (Rome, 1912)
Att. 8	*Treize livres de motets parus chez Pierre Attaingnant en 1534 et 1535*, 8, ed. A. Tillman Merritt (Monaco, 1962)
Caeremoniale	*Caeremoniale rituum sacrorum ecclesiae S. Marci Venetiarum* of Bartholomeo Bonifacio, 1564 (Venice, Biblioteca Nazionale Marciana, Cod. Lat. III–172 [=2276])
Chev.	Ulysse Chevalier, *Repertorium Hymnologicum*, 6 vols. (Louvain, 1892–1910)
Gombert OO	*Nicolai Gombert Opera omnia*, 8 and 10, ed. Joseph Schmidt-Görg (Corpus mensurabilis musicae, 6; American Institute of Musicology, 1970–5)
Jacquet OO	*Jacquet of Mantua (1483-1559) Opera omnia*, 5, ed. George Nugent (Corpus mensurabilis musicae, 54; American Institute of Musicology, 1986)
Kabis	Sister Mary Elise Kabis, 'The Works of Johannes Richafort' (Ph.D. diss., New York University, 1957)
Lasso *Werke*	*Orlando di Lasso, Sämmtliche Werke*, ed. F. X. Haberl and A. Sandberger (Leipzig, 1894–1926)
L.R.	*Liber Responsorialis* (Solesmes, 1895)

L.U.

Liber Usualis (Tournai, New York, 1961)

Lucca Ant.

Antiphonaire monastique . . . de Lucques (Paléographie musicale, 9; Tournai, 1906)

Lupi OO

Johannis Lupi Opera omnia, 1, ed. Bonnie J. Blackburn (Corpus mensurabilis musicae, 84; American Institute of Musicology, 1980)

Macey

Patrick Macey, 'Savonarola and the Sixteenth-Century Motet', *Journal of the American Musicological Society*, 36 (1983), 422–52

Morales OO

Cristóbal de Morales, Opera omnia, 2, ed. Higinio Anglés (Monumentos de la Música Española, 13; Barcelona, 1953)

Ordinarium

Ordinarium divini officii iuxta consuetudinem Cathedralis Ecclesiae Tarvisinae, MS copied in 1524 (Treviso, Biblioteca Capitolare)

Palestrina *Opere*

Le Opere complete di Giovanni Pierluigi da Palestrina, 7 and 8, ed. Raffaele Casimiri (Rome, 1940)

Paolucci

Giuseppe Paolucci, *Arte Pratica di contrappunto dimostrata con essempi di vari autori*, 3 vols. (Venice, 1765–72)

Phinot OO

Dominici Phinot Opera omnia, 1, ed. Janez Höfler (Corpus mensurabilis musicae, 59; American Institute of Musicology, 1972)

Proc. Mon.

Processionale monasticum . . . Ordinis Sancti Benedicti (Solesmes, 1893)

Rore OO

Cipriani Rore Opera omnia, 1 and 6, ed. Bernhard Meier (Corpus mensurabilis musicae, 14; American Institute of Musicology, 1959 and 1975)

Smijers

A. Smijers, ed., *Werken van Josquin des Prés, Motetten*, Bundel 11 (Amsterdam, 1954)

Sparks

Edgar H. Sparks, *The Music of Noel Bauldeweyn* (Studies and Documents, 6; American Musicological Society, 1972)

Stäblein

Bruno Stäblein, ed., *Hymnen (I). Die mittelalterlichen Hymnen des Abendlandes* (Monumenta monodica medii aevi, 1; Kassel and Basel, 1956)

Torchi

L'arte musicale in Italia, 1, ed. Luigi Torchi (Milan, n.d.)

V.P.	*Variae preces* (Solesmes, 1901)
Verdelot OO	*Philippe Verdelot, Opera omnia,* 2, ed. Anne-Marie Bragard (Corpus mensurabilis musicae, 28; American Institute of Musicology, 1973)
Willaert OO	*Adriani Willaert Opera omnia,* 3, 5, 13, ed. Hermann Zenck and Walter Gerstenberg (Corpus mensurabilis musicae, 3; American Institute of Musicology, 1950–66)
Worc. Ant.	*Antiphonaire monastique . . . de Worcester* (Paléographie musicale, 12; Tournai, 1922)

Manuscript 29
Inventory derived from the card catalogue of Giovanni D'Alessi in the Biblioteca Capitolare, Treviso

1 Franc(esco) Patav(ino) [Santacroce], *Magnum misterium*, 5vv

2 Finot, *Surge illuminare Jerus(alem)*, 2.p. *Omnes de Saba*, 5vv

3 Morales, *Cum natus esset* 5vv, 2.p. *At illi dixerunt* 4vv, 3.p. *Et ecce stella*, 5vv

4 Finot, *Descendit spiritus [sanctus]*, 5vv

5 Morales, *Antoni pater inclite*, 5vv

6 Jachet, *O lampas ardens*, 5vv

7 Gombert, *Egregie martir Sebast(iane)*, 2.p. *Socius enim*, 5vv

8 Archadelt, *Diem festum sacratissime*, 2.p. *Dexteram eius*, 5vv

9 Gislinus [Danckerts], *Tu es vas electionis*, 2.p. *Intercede pro nobis*, 5vv

10 Scaffen, *Senex puerum portabat*, 5vv

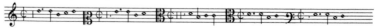

Feast	Text[1]	Probable Source	Remarks
Christmas (25 December)	Second antiphon, second Nocturn, Octave of Epiphany (V.P. 96)	Treviso 30, no. 5	
Epiphany (6 January)	Fourth and fifth responsories (without versus) at Matins (L.R. 75–6)	Gardane 1549[6], p. 1	The liturgical text begins with 'Illuminare', as does the concordance in Gardane 1549[6].
Epiphany (6 January)	Gospel (L.U. 461)	Treviso 30, no. 2	Mod. ed. Morales OO 2, p. 79.
Octave of Epiphany (13 January)	Antiphon to the Magnificat, 1st Vespers	Phinot 1552, p. 7	Contrafactum of *Tanto tempore* (see no. 24). Mod. ed. Phinot OO 1, p. 23.
St Anthony, Abbot (17 January)	First strophe of hymn 'de S. Antonio Thebano' (Chev. 1203)	Treviso 30, no. 13	
St Anthony, Abbot (17 January)		Gardane 1553[17], p. 36	Mod. ed. Jacquet OO 5, p. 190. The liturgical position confirms Nugent's suggestion that the saint is Anthony, Abbot, not Anthony of Padua.
SS Fabian and Sebastian, Martyrs (20 January)	Not in 1562 breviary. Responsory (Proc. Mon. 127)	Moderne 1532[9], p. 9 (without name of saint)	Mod. ed. Gombert OO 10, p. 67.
St Agnes, Virgin and Martyr (21 January)	First and second responsories (without versus) at Matins	Treviso 30, no. 4	Contrafactum of *Signum salutis pone Domine*, attributed to Archadelt in Treviso 30 but to Crecquillon in Kriesstein 1545[3], no. 30, and Montanus & Neuber 1555[11], no. 18.
Conversion of St Paul, Apostle (25 January)	Fourth responsory at Matins (Proc. Mon. 162)	Phinot 1552, p. 2	Contrafactum of Phinot's *Tua est potentia*. Mod. ed. Phinot OO 1, p. 5.
Purification of the B.V.M. (2 February)	Antiphon to the Magnificat, 1st Vespers (Ant. Mon. 801)		

[1] Liturgical placement follows that of the *Breviarium Romanum* of 1562 (see p.18, note d), which sometimes differs from current practice; for changes in the 1568 breviary, see Chapter 2, note 24 above. Texts cited from the *Ordinarium* (see p. 18, note a) were found only in the liturgy of Treviso; those cited from the *Caeremoniale* (see p.18, note b) occur in the liturgy of St Mark's.

11 Corvus, *Hodie beata Virgo [Maria puerum]*, 5vv

12 Comes, *Ave martir egregie [o salutaris medice]*, 5vv

13 Finot, *Agatha lętissime*, 2.p. *Nobilissimis orta natalibus*, 5vv

14 Comes, *Virgo martir*, 2.p. *Ora pro nobis*, 5vv

15 Gombert, *Tu es Petrus*, 2.p. *Quodcumque ligaveris*, 5vv

16 Gombert, *Sancte Gregori*, 5vv

17 Jachet, *O felix custos*, 5vv

18 Gombert, *Suscipe verbum [Virgo Maria]*, 2.p. *Paries quidem*, 5vv

19 Finot, *Gabriel nunciavit Mariae*, 2.p. *Pneumatis latet*, 5vv

20 Jo. Lupi, *Sancte Marce evang(elista)*, 5vv

Feast	Text	Probable Source	Remarks
Purification of the B.V.M. (2 February)	Antiphon to the Magnificat, 2nd Vespers (Ant. Mon. 805)	Corvus 1555, p. 16	
St Blaise, Bishop and Martyr (3 February)		Comes 1547, p. 7	The text begins 'O martir' in Comes 1547 and Treviso 8, f. 112v.
St Agatha, Virgin and Martyr (5 February)	Second responsory at Matins	Phinot 1552, p. 37	Contrafactum of *Auribus percipe Domine*. Mod. ed. Phinot OO 1, p. 140.
St Apollonia, Virgin and Martyr (9 February)		Comes 1547, p. 15	Contrafactum of *Domine ne longe facias*.
Chair of St Peter at Antioch (22 February)	Third responsory at Matins (L.R. 360)		Attributed to Morales in Scotto 1541[3], no. 14, Kriesstein 1545[3], no. 28 (but to Ghiselinus Danckerts in Bassus), Susato 1546[7], f. 13v, and Toledo 17, f. 74v; attributed to Simon Moreau in Phalèse 1553[11], no. 3; anon. in Florence 11, f. 126v, and Susato 1557[3], f. 16. Mod. ed. Morales OO 2, p. 149.
St Gregory I, Pope, Confessor and Doctor of the Church (12 March)		Lupi 1542, f. 14v	Contrafactum of *Sancti per fidem*, 2.p. of Lupi's *Isti sunt viri sancti*. Mod. ed. Lupi OO 1, p. 111.
St Joseph, Spouse of the B.V.M. (19 March)	Antiphon to the Magnificat, 2nd Vespers	Gardane 1553[17], p. 5	Contrafactum of *O fides spei columen*, 2.p. of *O quam praeclara sunt*, as is no. 67. Mod. ed. Jacquet OO 5, p. 30.
Annunciation of the B.V.M. (25 March)	Third responsory at Matins (Proc. Mon. 245)	Moderne 1532[9], p. 32	Mod. ed. Gombert OO 10, p. 73.
Annunciation of the B.V.M. (25 March)		Moderne 1538[2], p. 6	Attributed to Gombert in Moderne. Mod. ed. Gombert OO 10, p. 91.
St Mark, Evangelist (25 April)		Moderne 1538[2], p. 2, or Lupi 1542, f. 9v	Contrafactum of *Quae est ista*, 2.p. of *Vidi speciosam sicut columbam*. Mod. ed. Lupi OO 1, p. 70.

21 Joseph Zarlinus, *Beatissimus Marcus [discipulus]*, 2.p. *Accepto evangelio*, 5vv

22 [Verdelot], *Ave Confessor gloriose Liberalis*, 5vv

23 Innocentius Alberti, *Hic est dies egregius sanctissimi Liberalis*, 2.p. *Hodie beatum Liberalem*, 5vv

24 Finot dominicus, *Tanto tempore [vobiscum sum]*, 5vv

*Should be alto clef

25 Jachet Berchem, *In illo tempore [dixit Jesus]*, 2.p. *Domine ostende nobis*, 5vv

26 Joannes Baptista Corvus Novocomensis, *Nos autem gloriari oportet*, 5vv

27 Angeli Petraloysii proenestini, *Circuire possum Domine*, 2.p. *In hac cruce*, 5vv

28 Tugdual, *Gloriosum diem*, 2.p. *Tropheum crucis*, 6vv

Canon in diapente
supra Gloriosum

29 Gulielmi Textoris, *In ferventis olei*, 5vv

30 Bernardini Garilli, *Dum sacrum misterium*, 5vv

Feast	Text	Probable Source	Remarks
St Mark, Evangelist (25 April)	Responsory, 1st Vespers (*Ordinarium*, f. 109v; a responsory follows the 'historia')	Zarlino 1549, p. 16	
St Liberalis, Confessor (27 April)	Antiphon to the Magnificat, 1st Vespers (*Ordinarium*, f. 110v)	Moderne 1538[2], p. 37	Contrafactum of *Educes me de laqueo*, 2.p. of Verdelot's *In te Domine speravi*. Mod. ed. Verdelot OO 2, p. 32.
St Liberalis, Confessor (27 April)			
SS Philip and James, Apostles (1 May)	Third antiphon at Lauds (Ant. Mon. 893)	Phinot 1552, p. 7	See also no. 4. Mod. ed. Phinot OO 1, p. 23.
SS Philip and James, Apostles (1 May)	1.p.: beginning of Gospel at Mass (L.U. 1465c). 2.p.: first antiphon at Lauds (Ant. Mon. 893)	Gardane 1553[17], p. 2	
Finding of the Holy Cross (3 May)	Second responsory at Matins (without versus), Feast of Exaltation of the Holy Cross, 14 September (Worc. Ant. 309)	Corvus 1555, p. 13	
Finding of the Holy Cross (3 May)		Palestrina 1572, no. 12	Mod. ed. Palestrina *Opere*, 7, p. 70.
Finding of the Holy Cross (3 May)	First responsory at Matins and first responsory at Matins in Feast of Exaltation of the Holy Cross (without versus)	Treviso 5, no. 9 (anon.)	
St John before the Lateran Gate (6 May)	Antiphon to the Magnificat, 1st Vespers (Ant. Mon. 904)	Treviso 30, no. 17	Contrafactum of *Domine ante te.*
Victory of St Michael, Archangel (8 May)	Antiphon to the Magnificat, 1st Vespers (L.U. 1652)	Garulli 1562, p. 11	

31 Bernardini Garulli, *Gaudent in caelis,* 5vv

32 Adriani Will(aert), *O sodales Sancti Vindemialis et Florentii,* 5vv

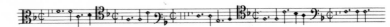

33 Adrianus willaert, *O proles hispaniae,* 6vv

Canon: Fuga trium Temporum
in diapente intensum

34 Metre Jan, *Da ecclesię tuę,* 5vv

Canon. Ut iacet in primo In
quarta quoque secundo idipsum
repetens, pausas liquenda priores

35 Jo. Animuccia florentinus, *Fuit homo missus a Deo,* 5vv

36 Joannes Continus, *Hic est precursor dilectus,* 6vv

Resolutio ex Tenore   Fuga duplex: Primo unius
Temporis, secundo duorum
temporum in diapente remissum

37 Gomberth, *Surge Petre [et indue te],* 2.p. *Angelus Domini [astitit],* 5vv

38 Jo. Petraloysius Proenestinus, *Tu es Petrus,* 2.p. *Quodcumque ligaveris,* 6vv

39 Lafage, *Sancte Paule Apostole,* 5vv

Resolutio   Canon in diapente remissum

Feast	Text	Probable Source	Remarks
SS Florentius and Vindemialis, Confessors (1 June)	Possibly antiphon to the Magnificat, 2nd Vespers, Common of Two or More Martyrs, with names of saints inserted (L.U. 1160). From an inventory of 1427 we know that the cathedral possessed two antiphoners that began 'In Nativitate Ss. Confessorum Florentii et Vindimialis: gaudent in cellis'; see D'Alessi, La Cappella musicale, p. 255.	Garulli 1562, p. 2	
SS Florentius and Vindemialis, Confessors (1 June)	Antiphon to the Magnificat, 1st and 2nd Vespers (Ordinarium, f. 114)	Willaert 1559, no. 6	Contrafactum of 1.p. of Miserere nostri Deus. Mod. ed. Willaert OO 5, p. 56.
St Anthony of Padua, Confessor and Doctor of the Church (13 June)	Antiphon to the Magnificat, 1st Vespers		Concordances in Modena C 314, p. 64, Lucca 775, f. 59v, and Wolfenbüttel 293, no. 33.
SS Vitus, Modestus and Crescentia, Martyrs (15 June)	Oratio (Ant. Mon. 917)	Treviso 7, f. 43v (anon.)	
Nativity of St John the Baptist (24 June)	Short responsory at Lauds (Ant. Mon. 925)	Animuccia 1552, no. 17	
Nativity of St John the Baptist (24 June)	Fifth responsory at Matins (without versus) (L.R. 353)	Continus 1560/1, p. 9	
SS Peter and Paul, Apostles (29 June)	Fifth responsory at Matins (L.R. 363)	Gombert 1541 or 1550, no. 17	Mod. ed. Gombert OO 8, p. 107.
SS Peter and Paul, Apostles (29 June)	Third responsory at Matins (L.R. 360)	Palestrina 1572, no. 24	Mod. ed. Palestrina Opere 7, p. 162.
SS Peter and Paul, Apostles (29 June)	Antiphon to the Magnificat, 1st Vespers (L.U. 1350)	Treviso 6, no. 7 (anon.)	Contrafactum of Partus et integritas (concordances in C.S. 38, f. 40; Antico 1521[5], f. 13v; anon. in Bologna SP 31, f. 130v). Treviso 6 has the contrafactum text.

40   Joannes Continus, *Deus cuius dextera*, 5vv

41   Adrianus Vuillart, *[O] Christi martir sancte Chiliane*, 5vv

42   Jo. Continus, *Intervenientibus Domine [sanctis martyribus tuis]*, 5vv

43   Cyprianus Rore, *Mulier quae erat*, 5vv

44   M. Jan, *Sancte Jacobe Apostole*, 2.p. *O lux et decus Hispaniae*, 5vv

Pro prima parte descende gradatim
pro secunda parte scande gradatim

45   Gomberth, *O felix Anna [ex stirpe David]*, 2.p. *O Anna purissima*, 5vv

46   Adrianus vuillart, *Benedictus redemptor [omnium]*, 2.p. *Magne pater sancte Dominice*, 5vv

47   [Bartholomeus Comes] Gallicus, *Assumpsit Jesus [Petrum, et Jacobum, et Joannem]*, 5vv

48   Adrianus vuillaert, *Beatus Laurentius [orabat dicens]*, 6vv

Canon in diapente
remissum

49   Joannes Continus, *O quam magnificum*, 5vv

50   Adrianus, *Beatus Bernardus*, 5vv

51   [Contino], *Omnipotens sempiterne Deus*, 5vv

Feast	Text	Probable Source	Remarks
Octave of SS Peter and Paul, Apostles (6 July)	Oratio (Ant. Mon. 959)	Continus 1560/1, p. 22	Contrafactum of *Deus qui nobis sub sacramento*.
St Kylianus and Companions (8 July)	Antiphon to the Magnificat, 1st Vespers (*Ordinarium*, f. 120v)	Willaert 1559, no. 6	Contrafactum of 1.p. of *Più volte già dal bel sembiante*. Mod. ed. Willaert OO 13, p. 19.
SS Hermacoras and Fortunatus, Martyrs (12 July)	Oratio (*Ordinarium*, f. 121)	Continus 1560/1, p. 29	Contrafactum of *O admirabile commercium*.
St Mary Magdalene, Penitent (22 July)	Antiphon to the Magnificat (Ant. Mon. 978)	Rore 1545, p. 32	Contrafactum of 1.p. of *Domine quis habitabit*. Mod. ed. Rore OO 1, p. 104.
St James, Apostle (25 July)		Treviso 36, f. 15v	
St Anne, Mother of the B.V.M. (26 July)		Gombert 1541 or 1550, no. 15	Mod. ed. Gombert OO 8, p. 96.
St Dominic, Confessor (4 August)		Gardane 1544[6], p. 15	
Transfiguration of Our Lord Jesus Christ (6 August)	First antiphon at Lauds (Ant. Mon. 998)	Comes 1547, p. 20	1.p. only.
St Lawrence, Martyr (10 August)	Fifth antiphon at Lauds (Ant. Mon. 1006)	Gardane 1542[10], p. 20	Mod. ed. Willaert OO 4, p. 44.
St Roch (16 August)	Communion (*Acta Sanctorum 37*, 390)	Continus 1560/1, p. 16	Contrafactum of 1.p. of *Texebat viridem cloris*. See also no. 66.
St Bernard of Clairvaux, Abbot, Confessor, and Doctor of the Church (20 August)	Antiphon to the Magnificat (*Ordinarium*, f. 128)	Willaert 1539 or 1550, no. 6	Contrafactum of *Domine Jesu Christe fili dei*. Mod. ed. Willaert OO 3, p. 31.
St Bartholomew, Apostle (24 August)	Oratio (Ant. Mon. 1024)	Continus 1560/1, p. 1	Contrafactum of 1.p. of *O magnum mysterium*.

52 Maistre Jannes, *Praesul sanctissime Augustine*, 6vv

Canon in diapente
intensum

53 [Comes], *Misit rex incredulus*, 2.p. *Herodes enim*, 5vv

* should be
mezzo soprano
clef

54 [Contino], *Beati evangeliste Mathei*, 5vv

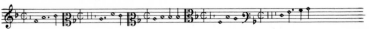

55 M. Jann(es), *Clementissime Deus*, 2.p. *Tuque sacer Hieronime*, 5vv

56 Adrianus, *Sancte Francisce [propere veni]*, 6vv

Fuga quattuor temporum
in diapente intensum

57 [Willaert], *Gaudeamus*, 2.p. *Cantemus*, 5vv

58 Maistre Jann(es), *Sacrę legis [Christianae]*, 2.p. *Precamur [ergo supplices]*, 5vv

59 Adrianus, *Gaudeamus omnes*, 5vv

60 [Contino], *Deus qui nos*, 5vv

61 Comes, *Te gloriosus Apostolorum*, 5vv

62 Dominicus Finot, *O quam gloriosum est regnum*, 5vv

Feast	Text	Probable Source	Remarks
St Augustine, Bishop, Confessor and Doctor of the Church (28 August)	Antiphon to the Benedictus, Second Translation of St Augustine (28 February) (Breviarium Romanum, Venice, 1486)	Treviso 4, no. 15	
Beheading of St John the Baptist (29 August)	Antiphon to the Magnificat, 2nd Vespers, and first antiphon at Lauds (Ant. Mon. 1029, 1026)	Comes 1547, p. 4	Contrafactum of *Cum iocunditate*; see II/15.
St Matthew, Apostle and Evangelist (21 September)	Oratio (Ant. Mon. 1053)	Continus 1560/2, p. 4	Contrafactum of 1.p. of *Assumpta est Maria*.
St Jerome, Priest, Confessor and Doctor of the Church (30 September)		Treviso 30, no. 12	
St Francis, Confessor (4 October)	Antiphon to the Magnificat in the Suffragia Sanctorum		Concordances in Wolfenbüttel 293, no. 32, and Lucca 775, f. 58v.
St Justina (7 October)		Willaert 1559, no. 7	Contrafactum of *Quando fra l'altre donne*. Mod. ed. Willaert OO 13, p. 23.
St Luke, Evangelist (18 October)		Treviso 5, no. 50 (anon.)	
11,000 Virgins, Martyrs (21 October)		Willaert 1559, no. 6	Contrafactum of *Alleva manum*, 2.p. of *Miserere nostri Deus* (cf. no. 32). Mod. ed. Willaert OO 5, p. 56.
SS Simon and Jude, Apostles (28 October)	Oratio (Ant. Mon. 1098)	Continus 1560/1, p. 20	Contrafactum of 1.p. of *Austriae stirpis*.
All Saints (1 November)	Antiphon to the Benedictus (Ant. Mon. 1105)	Comes 1547, p. 23	
All Saints (1 November)	Antiphon to the Magnificat, 2nd Vespers (Ant. Mon. 1107)	Phinot 1552, p. 26	Mod. ed. Phinot OO 1, p. 100.

63   Jo. Continus, *Sancti Dei omnes*, 5vv

64   Dominicus Finot, *Te gloriosus Apostolorum*, 5vv

65   Jo. Continus, *O quam gloriosum [est regnum]*, 6vv

Canon in diapente intensum   * Orig. : E

66   [Contino], *Gaude et laetare*, 2.p. *Gaude igitur Tarvisina civitas*, 5vv

67   [Jachet], *O praesul venerabilis*, 5vv

68   Continus, *O beatum virum*, 5vv

69   Adrianus, *O beatum pontificem*, 6vv

Canon in subdiapente

70   Proenestini, *Beatus dei famulus*, 2.p. *Gaude Tarvisina civitas*, 5vv

71   Petri Antonij Spalenza, *Deus alma spes*, 5vv

72   Joannes Continus, *Prudens et vigilans*, 5vv

73   M. Jannes, *Ambulans Jesus [iuxta mare]*, 2.p. *[At illi continuo] relictis*, 5vv

74   Jo. Petraloysii proenestini, *O Sancte praesul Nicolae*, 2.p. *Gaude praesul optime*, 5vv

Feast	Text	Probable Source	Remarks
All Saints (1 November)	Not in 1562 breviary. Three antiphons (Ant. Rom. [90], L.R. 385, L.U. 1160)	Continus 1560/1, p. 26	
All Saints (1 November)	See no. 61	Phinot 1552, p. 27	Mod. ed. Phinot OO 1, p. 104.
All Saints (1 November)	See no. 62	Continus 1560/3, p. 8	
St Prosdocimus, Confessor (7 November)		Continus 1560/1, p. 16	Contrafactum of *Texebat viridem cloris*, as is no. 49.
St Prosdocimus, Confessor (7 November)		Gardane 1553[17], p. 5	Contrafactum of *O fides spei columen*, 2.p. of *O quam praeclara sunt*, as is no. 17. Mod. ed. Jacquet OO 5, p. 30.
St Martin, Bishop and Confessor (11 November)	Antiphon to the Magnificat, 1st Vespers (Ant. Mon. 1114)	Continus 1560/1, p. 15	
St Martin, Bishop and Confessor (11 November)	Antiphon to the Magnificat, 2nd Vespers (Ant. Mon. 1118)	Gardane 1542[10], p. 14	Mod. ed. Willaert OO 4, p. 28.
SS Theonistus, Tabra and Tabrata (22 November)	Antiphon at Lauds and Hours (*Ordinarium*, f. 139v)	Palestrina 1572, no. 13	Contrafactum of *Gaude Barbara*. Mod. ed. Palestrina *Opere* 7, p. 78.
SS Theonistus, Tabra and Tabrata (22 November)	Antiphon to the Magnificat, 1st Vespers (*Ordinarium*, f. 139v)		Transcription below, Appendix, no. 2.
St Catherine, Virgin and Martyr (25 November)	Antiphon to the Benedictus	Continus 1560/1, p. 6	
St Andrew, Apostle (30 November)	Gospel (L.U. 1306)	Treviso 4, no. 60	Concordance in Treviso 36, f. 15, and other sources.
St Nicholas, Bishop and Confessor (6 December)		Palestrina 1575, no. 16	Mod. ed. Palestrina *Opere* 8, p. 102.

75 Perissonus, *Ave ignea columna*, 2.p. *O Dei electe*, 5vv

76 Jo. Petraloysius proenestinus, *Columna es [immobilis]*, 6vv

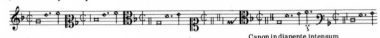

Canon in diapente intensum

77 Gomberth, *In tua pacientia*, 2.p. *Lucia virgo*, 5vv

78 Continus, *Quia vidisti me Thoma*, 2.p. *Infer digitum*, 5vv

79 Cypriani Rore, *Hodie scietis*, 5vv

80 Continus, *Hodie Christus natus est*, 5vv

81 Continus, *Patefactę sunt ianuę*, 2.p. *Mortem enim*, 5vv

82 Proenestinus, *In medio ecclesiae*, 2.p. *Iucunditatem [et exultationem]*, 5vv

83 Continus, *Innocentes pro Christo*, 5vv

84 Proenestinus, *Silvester beatissimus*, 5vv

Feast	Text	Probable Source	Remarks
St Ambrose, Bishop, Confessor, and Doctor of the Church (7 December)		Gardane 1549[8], p. 3	Contrafactum of *Ad te Domine animam meam.*
St Lucy, Virgin and Martyr (13 December)	Antiphon to the Benedictus (Ant. Mon. 771)	Palestrina 1575, no. 23	Mod. ed. Palestrina *Opere* 8, p. 151.
St Lucy, Virgin and Martyr (13 December)	Antiphon to the Magnificat, 1st Vespers, and second antiphon at Lauds (Ant. Mon. 769, 770)	Gombert 1552, p. 19	Contrafactum of *Veni dilecta mea.* Mod. ed. Gombert OO 8, p. 132.
St Thomas, Apostle (21 December)	1.p.: Antiphon to the Magnificat, 1st and 2nd Vespers (Ant. Mon. 774)	Continus 1560/1, p. 27	Contrafactum of *Maria stabat ad monumentum.*
Vigil of the Nativity of Our Lord (24 December)	Second Antiphon at Lauds (Ant. Mon. 232)	Rore 1545, p. 10	Contrafactum of *Pulchrior italicis.* Mod. ed. Rore OO 1, p. 48.
Nativity of Our Lord (25 December)	Antiphon to the Magnificat, 2nd Vespers (Ant. Mon. 249)	Continus 1560/1, p. 23	
St Stephen, Protomartyr (26 December)	Eighth responsory at Matins (Lucca Ant. 46)	Continus 1560/1, p. 10	Contrafactum of *Tempus est ut revertar.*
St John, Apostle and Evangelist (27 December)	Sixth responsory at Matins (L.R. 203)	Palestrina 1572, no. 1	Contrafactum of *O virgo simul et mater* (see II/32). Mod. ed. Palestrina *Opere* 7, p. 1. The motet has one *pars.* Since D'Alessi did not give musical incipits for the *secundae partes*, it is not possible to tell whether the present motet was divided in two for the contrafactum or whether the 2.p. was based on another motet.
Holy Innocents, Martyrs (28 December)	Antiphon to the Magnificat (Ant. Mon. 264)	Continus 1560/2, p. 3	
St Silvester, Pope and Confessor (31 December)	Not in 1562 breviary. Antiphon to the Magnificat (*Caeremoniale*, f. 22v)	Palestrina 1572, no. 16	Contrafactum of *Peccantem me quotidie.* Mod. ed. Palestrina *Opere* 7, p. 98.

85 Continus, *Benedictus qui venit*, 5vv

86 Orlandi Lassi, *Videntes stellam [Magi gavisi sunt]*, 2.p. *Et apertis thesauris*, 5vv

87 Orlandi Lassi, *Antoni pater*, 5vv

88 Cyprianus Rore, *Petre amas me*, 2.p. *Simon Joannis*, 5vv

89 Joseph Zarlinus, *Sebastianus Dei cultor*, 6vv

Canon in diapente
intenso ut patet

90 Jachet, *Stans beata Agnes*, 5vv

91 Franc(isci) portinarii, *Laudemus Deum*, 2.p. *Hic est vas*, 5vv

92 Jo. Naschi (Giov. Nasco in Altus), *Magnificemus [Deum salvatorem]*, 5vv

93 Orlandi Lassi, *Elegit te Dominus*, 2.p. *Imola Deo*, 5vv

94 Continus, *Deus qui beatum*, 5vv

95 Orlandi Lassi, *O lux Italiae*, 5vv

96 Cypriani Rore, *O Gregori*, 5vv

Feast	Text	Probable Source	Remarks
Circumcision of Our Lord (1 January)	Third responsory at Matins, without versus	Continus 1560/1, p. 4	Contrafactum of 1.p. of *Letentur celi.*
Epiphany (6 January)	Eighth responsory at Matins, with different versus (L.R. 79)	Lassus 1562, no. 4	Mod. ed. Lasso *Werke* 5, p. 22.
St Anthony, Abbot (17 January)	See no. 5	Lassus 1562, no. 15	Contrafactum of *Surrexit pastor bonus.* Mod. ed. Lasso *Werke* 5, p. 57.
Chair of St Peter at Rome (18 January)	Not in 1562 breviary. Responsory (L.R. 361)	Rore 1545, p. 12	Contrafactum of *In Domino confido.* Mod. ed. Rore OO 1, p. 51.
SS Fabian and Sebastian, Martyrs (20 January)	Antiphon at Vespers (*Ordinarium*, f. 98)	Zarlino 1566, no. 11	
St Agnes, Virgin and Martyr (21 January)	Antiphon to the Magnificat, 2nd Vespers (Ant. Mon. 789)	Gardane 1549[8], p. 26	Contrafactum of *Enceladi ceique soror.*
Conversion of St Paul, Apostle (25 January)	1.p.: Invitatory (L.U. 432)	Portinaro 1548, p. 6	Contrafactum of *Sancta et immaculata.*
St Blaise, Bishop and Martyr (3 February)		Treviso 8, f. 110	
Chair of St Peter at Antioch (22 February)	Eighth responsory at Matins (L.R. 204)	Lassus 1562, no. 23	Contrafactum of *Illustra faciem tuam.* Mod. ed. Lasso *Werke* 9, p. 77.
St Matthias, Apostle (24 February)	Oratio (Ant. Mon. 827)	Continus 1560/1, p. 7	Contrafactum of *Ave vivens hostia.*
St Thomas Aquinas, Confessor and Doctor of the Church (10 March)		Lassus 1562, no. 11	Contrafactum of *Veni in hortum meum.* Mod. ed. Lasso *Werke* 5, p. 120.
St Gregory the Great, Pope, Confessor and Doctor of the Church (12 March)	Not in 1562 breviary. Antiphon (Proc. Mon. 141)	Rore 1545, p. 24	Contrafactum of 1.p. of *Cantantibus organis.* Mod. ed. Rore OO 1, p. 79.

97 Bernardini Garilli, *Vocatus Joseph*, 2.p. *Introducit Jesus*, 5vv

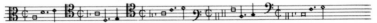

98 Continus, *Laudemus Dominum*, 2.p. *Benedictum sit*, 5vv

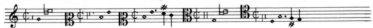

99 Josephi Zarlini, *Hodie Sanctus Benedictus*, 5vv

100 Jo. petraloysij proenestini, *Tradent enim vos*, 5vv

101 Gomberth, *Venite ad me [omnes qui laboratis]*, 5vv

102 Orlandi Lassi, *Non vos me elegistis*, 5vv

103 *Virtute magna [reddebant]*, 2.p. *Repleti quidem*, 5vv

104 Jo. petraloysij proenestini, *Corona aurea [super caput eius]*, 2.p. *Domine praevenisti*, 5vv

105 Joannis Continus, *Iste Sanctus [pro lege Dei]*, 5vv

106 Orlandi Lassi, *Qui vult venire*, 5vv

Feast	Text	Probable Source	Remarks
St Joseph, Spouse of the B.V.M. (19 March)	Ninth responsory at Matins	Garulli 1562, p. 9	
St Joachim, Father of the B.V.M. (20 March)	1.p.: possibly Invitatory (L.R. 435)	Continus 1560/2, p. 20	Contrafactum of *Surge Petre*. (This motet is erroneously attributed to Jachet in Modena C 313, p. 72; it was probably confused with Jachet's 6-voice *Surge Petre* found in the Vallicelliana MS and other sources.)
St Benedict, Abbot (21 March)	Not in 1562 breviary. Antiphon to the Magnificat, 2nd Vespers (Ant. Mon. 857)	Zarlino 1549, p. 21	Contrafactum of *Clodia quem genuit*.
Common of Apostles and Evangelists	Antiphon to the Magnificat, 1st Vespers (Ant. Mon. 621)	Palestrina 1575, no. 12	Mod. ed. Palestrina *Opere* 8, p. 75.
Common of Apostles	Matthew 11:28–30	Gombert 1541 or 1550, no. 12	Mod. ed. Gombert OO 8, p. 80.
Common of Apostles	Not in 1562 breviary. Antiphon (Worc. Ant. 307)	Lassus 1562, no. 25	Mod. ed. Lasso *Werke* 5, p. 141.
Common of Apostles in Paschaltide	First responsory at Matins, third feria after Easter (L.R. 87)	Gardane 1549[6], p. 30	Attributed to Rore in *Cipriani de Rore Sacrae Cantiones . . . cum quinque, sex et septem vocibus* (Venice: Gardano, 1595). Mod. ed. Rore OO 6, p. 153.
Common of One Martyr	Seventh responsory at Matins (L.R. 158)	Palestrina 1572, no. 3	Mod. ed. Palestrina *Opere* 7, p. 13.
Common of One Martyr	Antiphon to the Magnificat, 1st Vespers (Ant. Mon. 639)	Continus 1560/2, no. 10	Contrafactum of 1.p. of *Ut te muneribus*.
Common of One Martyr	Antiphon to the Magnificat, 2nd Vespers (Ant. Mon. 644)	Lassus 1562, no. 1	Contrafactum of *Confitemini Domino*. Mod. ed. Lasso *Werke* 7, p. 131.

107 Jo. petraloysius proenestinus, *Filiae Jerusalem [venite et videte]*, 2.p. *Quoniam confortavit*, 5vv.

108 Dominicus Finot, *Istorum est enim regnum*, 5vv

109 Franc(iscus) Portinarus, *Absterget Deus [omnem lachrymam]*, 2.p. *Non exurient*, 5vv

110 Comes (Bartholomeus Comes in Altus, Tenor, Bassus), *Gauden[t] in coelis*, 5vv

111 Proenestini, *Haec est vera fraternitas*, 2.p. *Ecce quam bonum*, 5vv

112 Jo. Contini, *Sacerdos et pontifex*, 5vv

113 Gomberth, *Juravit dominus [et non paenitebit]*, 2.p. *Dixit Dominus*, 5vv

114 Joseph Zarlinus, *Amavit eum dominus*, 5vv

Resolutio   Fuga duorum temporum
                                               in diatessaron intensum

115 Franc(isci) portinarij, *Dum esset summus pontifex*, 5vv

116 Adriani will(aert), *O doctor optime*, 5vv

                              Resolutio   Fuga duorum temporum
                                               in diatessaron intensum

117 Jachet, *Similabo eum*, 5vv

     Fuga duorum temporum   Resolutio
     in diapente remissum

118 Continus, *Iste est qui ante Deum*, 2.p. *Iste est qui contempsit*, 5vv

Feast	Text	Probable Source	Remarks
Common of Apostles and Martyrs in Paschaltide	Not in 1562 breviary. Responsory (L.R. 169)	Palestrina 1575, no. 5	Contrafactum of *Angelus Domini descendit*. Mod. ed. Palestrina *Opere* 8, p. 23.
Common of Martyrs	Antiphon to the Magnificat, 1st Vespers (Ant. Mon. 647)	Phinot 1552, p. 32	Mod. ed. Phinot OO 1, p. 123.
Common of Martyrs	First responsory at Matins (L.R. 178)	Portinaro 1548, p. 3	
Common of Martyrs	Antiphon to the Magnificat, 2nd Vespers (Ant. Mon. 653)	Comes 1547, p. 25	
Common of Two or More Martyrs	Eighth responsory at Matins (Proc. Mon. 222)	Palestrina 1572, no. 10	Contrafactum of *Canite tuba in Sion*. Mod. ed. Palestrina *Opere* 7, p. 56.
Common of a Confessor Bishop	Antiphon to the Magnificat, 1st Vespers (Ant. Mon. 656)	Continus 1560/1, p. 18	Contrafactum of *Sanctorum martyrum tuorum*.
Common of a Confessor Bishop	Third responsory at Matins (L.R. 195)	Gombert 1541, no. 4	Contrafactum of *Caeciliam cantate*. Mod. ed. Gombert OO 8, p. 26.
Common of a Confessor Bishop	Antiphon to the Magnificat, 2nd Vespers (Ant. Mon. 663)	Zarlino 1549, p. 3	Contrafactum of *O beatum pontificem*.
Common of a Confessor Bishop	Antiphon to the Magnificat, 2nd Vespers (Ant. Mon. 663)	Portinaro 1548, p. 10	Contrafactum of *Da pacem*.
Common of Doctors	Antiphon to the Magnificat, 1st and 2nd Vespers (Ant. Mon. 665)	Gardane 1549[8], p. 37	Contrafactum of *Creator omnium Deus*.
Common of a Confessor not a Bishop	Antiphon to the Magnificat, 1st Vespers (Ant. Mon. 669)	Moderne 1542[5], p. 39	Contrafactum of *Repleatur os meum*. Mod. ed. Jacquet OO 5, p. 160. D'Alessi miscopied the bass from no. 114.
Common of a Confessor not a Bishop	Fourth responsory at Matins (L.R. 199)	Continus 1560/2, p. 18	Contrafactum of *O stupor et gaudium*.

119 Ciprianus Rore, *Hic vir [despiciens mundum]*, 5vv

120 Richaforth, *Veni sponsa Christi*, 5vv

121 Cyprianus Rore, *Prudentes virgines [aptate lampades]*, 5vv

122 Gomberth, *Veni electa mea*, 5vv

123 Cyprianus, *Regnum mundi*, 2.p. *Exultavit cor meum*, 5vv

124 *Veni sponsa Christi*, 5vv

125 Comes, *Domus mea [domus orationis]*, 2.p. *Petite et accipietis*, 5vv

126 Proenestinus, *Sanctificavit [Dominus tabernaculum]*, 5vv

127 Proenestinus, *O quam metuendus*, 5vv

128 Proenestinus, *Inclitę Sanctę Virginis [Catherinae]*, 5vv

129 Proenestinus, *Fuit homo missus*, 2.p. *Erat Joannes*, 5vv

130 Proenestinus, *O lux et decus Hispanię*, 2.p. *O singolare [sic] praesidium*, 5vv

Feast	Text	Probable Source	Remarks
Common of a Confessor not a Bishop	Antiphon to the Magnificat, 2nd Vespers (Ant. Mon. 675)	Gardane 1549[8], p. 27	Contrafactum of 1.p. of *Augustiae mihi*. Mod. ed. Rore OO 1, p. 147.
Common of Virgins	Antiphon to the Magnificat, 2nd Vespers (Ant. Mon. 682)		Mod. ed. Medici Codex, 4, p. 391. For concordances, see 3, p. 233.
Common of Two or More Virgin Martyrs	Antiphon to the Magnificat and Benedictus, 1st and 2nd Vespers and Lauds (Ant. Mon. 683)	Rore 1545, p. 16	Contrafactum of 1.p. of *Exaudiat me Dominus*. Mod. ed. Rore OO 1, p. 56.
Common of Virgins and Holy Women	Cf. responsory L.R. 216.	Gombert 1552, p. 30	Mod. ed. Gombert OO 8, p. 137 (with 2.p.).
Common of Holy Women	Eighth responsory at Matins (L.R. 227)	Rore 1545, p. 20	Contrafactum of *Usquequo Domine*. Mod. ed. Rore OO 1, p. 68.
Common of Virgins	See no. 120	Gardane 1549[6], p. 21	
Common of the Dedication of a Church	Seventh responsory at Matins (L.R. 241)	Comes 1547, p. 2	D'Alessi miscopied the tenor from no. 123.
Common of the Dedication of a Church	Antiphon to the Magnificat, 1st Vespers (Ant. Mon. 696)	Palestrina 1575, no. 13	Mod. ed. Palestrina *Opere* 8, p. 80.
Common of the Dedication of a Church	Antiphon to the Magnificat, 2nd Vespers (Ant. Mon. 702)	Palestrina 1575, no. 14	Mod. ed. Palestrina *Opere* 8, p. 85.
St Catherine, Virgin and Martyr (25 November)	Antiphon to the Magnificat, 1st Vespers	Palestrina 1575, no. 7	Mod. ed. Palestrina *Opere* 8, p. 45.
Nativity of St John the Baptist (24 June)	First responsory at Matins (L.R. 348)	Palestrina 1575, no. 8	Mod. ed. Palestrina *Opere* 8, p. 49.
St James, Apostle (25 July)		Palestrina 1575, no. 9	Mod. ed. Palestrina *Opere* 8, p. 57.

131   Proenestinus, *Praeceptor bonum est*, 2.p. *Non enim [sciebat]*, 5vv

132   Proenestinus, *Omnipotens sempiterne Deus*, 5vv

Second Series

All of these motets are for feasts of the B.V.M.

1   Jo. Nasco, *Inviolata [integra et casta es]*, 2.p. *Nostra ut pura*, 5vv

2   Jachet, *Descendi in hortum*, 6vv

Canon in diapente
superius

3   Jachet Berchem, *Qualis es dilecta mea*, 6vv

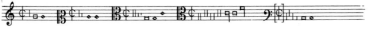

4   Cipriani Rore, *Gaude Maria [Virgo cunctas haereses]*, 2.p. *Gabrielem Archangelum*, 5vv

5   Franc(isci) portinarij, *Vidi speciosam [sicut columbam]*, 5vv

6   Adriani W(illaert), *O gloriosa domina*, 2.p. *Maria mater gratiae*, 6vv

Canon in diapente superius

7   Jachet, *Ave quam colunt angeli*, 2.p. *Audi quid [anxiusculis]*, 5vv

8   Adriani Will(aert), *Beata viscera [Mariae virginis]*, 6vv

Canon in dyapente
inferius

*Orig. : dotted
semibreve

9   *Sicut lilium [inter spinas]*, 5vv

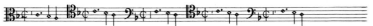

Feast	Text	Probable Source	Remarks
Transfiguration of Our Lord (6 August)	Fifth responsory at Matins	Palestrina 1575, no. 6	Contrafactum of *Congrega, Domine*. Mod. ed. Palestrina *Opere* 8, p. 35.
St Bartholomew, Apostle (24 August)	Oratio (Ant. Mon. 1024)	Palestrina 1575, no. 16	Mod. ed. Palestrina *Opere* 8, p. 98.
	Sequence (L.U. 1861)		Transcription below, Appendix, no. 4.
	Antiphon (Proc. Mon. 243)	Gardane 1539[3], p. 21	Mod. ed. Att. 8, p. 155.
		Gardane 1539[3], p. 6	
Annunciation of the B.V.M. (25 March)	Responsory (Proc. Mon. 146)	Rore 1545, p. 8	Mod. ed. Rore OO 1, p. 12.
Assumption of the B.V.M. (15 August)	First responsory (without versus) at Matins (L.R. 376)	Portinaro 1548, p. 17	
	Hymn (Ant. Rom. [Supplement], 46)	Gardane 1542[10], p. 24	Mod. ed. Willaert OO 4, p. 59.
		Gardane 1549[8], p. 32	
	Communion (L.U. 1268)	Gardane 1542[10], p. 40	Mod. ed. Willaert OO 4, p. 105.
Immaculate Conception of the B.V.M. (8 December)	Antiphon at 1st Vespers (Ant. Rom. [207])	Gardane 1549[6], p. 7	

10 Josephi Zarlini, *Ecce tu pulchra [es amica mea]*, 5vv

Resolutio ex tenore   Canon in diapason

11 Jachet, *Murus tuus dilecta*, 2.p. *Ego murus sum*, 6vv

Canon in diatessaron
superius

12 Cypriani Rore, *Si ignoras te [o pulchra]*, 2.p. *Surge propera [amica mea]*, 5vv

13 *Virgo Maria [speciosissima]*, 2.p. *Virgo Maria [virga Iesse florida]*, 5vv

14 Adriani Vuillart, *Ave Virgo sponsa [Dei]*, 2.p. *Igitur nos [merito]*, 6vv

Resolutio super Ave

15 Bartholomei Comitis Gallici, *Cum iucunditate [nativitatem]*, 2.p. *Corde et animo [Christo canamus]*, 5vv

16 Joseph Zarlini, *Virgo prudentissima*, 6vv

Canon in diapente
inferius

17 Jachet, *Alma redemptoris*, 2.p. *Tu quae genuisti*, 5vv

18 Arnoldi, *Rosa de spinis [protulit]*, 2.p. *Miranda salutatio*, 5vv

19 Dominici Finot, *Osculetur me [osculo oris sui]*, 5vv

20 Josephi Zarlini, *Adiuro vos*, 5vv

21 Francisci portinarij, *Sicut cedrus [exaltata sum]*, 2.p. *In plateis [sicut cinamomum]*, 5vv

Feast	Text	Probable Source	Remarks
	Two antiphons (Worc. Ant. 354, 162)	Zarlino 1549, p. 11	Mod. ed. Torchi 1, p. 79.
		Moderne 1542[5], p. 46	
	Song of Songs 1:7, 4:7, 2:10b, 14b	Rore 1545, p. 22	Mod. ed. Rore OO 1, p. 74.
		Gardane 1549[6], p. 14	
		Gardane 1542[10], p. 17	Mod. ed. Willaert OO 4, p. 37.
Nativity of the B.V.M. (8 September)	Fifth responsory at Matins	Comes 1547, p. 4	See also no. 53.
Assumption of the B.V.M. (15 August)	Antiphon to the Magnificat, 1st Vespers (L.U. 1600[2])	Zarlino 1566, no. 5	Mod. ed. Paolucci 2, p. 250.
	Antiphon, Sunday at Compline (L.U. 273)	Gardane 1553[17], p. 16, or Moderne 1532[9], p. 22	Mod. ed. Jacquet OO 5, p. 132.
Visitation of the B.V.M. (2 July)	Fifth responsory at Matins	Gardane 1549[6], p. 28	The composer is probably Ernold Caussin.
	Song of Songs 1:1–3a	Phinot 1552, p. 25	Mod. ed. Phinot OO 1, p. 95.
	Song of Songs 3:5–6	Gardane 1549[8], p. 16	
	Responsory (but not L.R. 252)	Portinaro 1548, p. 20	

22 Franc(isci) portinarij, *Benedicta et venerabilis*, 6vv

23 *Ave sanctissima Maria [Mater Dei]*, 5vv

24 Jo. Baptistę Corvi Novocomensis, *Surge propera amica mea*, 5vv

25 *Felix nanque es*, 2.p. *Ora pro populo*, 5vv

26 Josephi Zarlini, *Ave Regina coelorum*, 5vv

27 *Suscipe verbum [Virgo Maria]*, 5vv

28 Jachet, *Ave virgo gratiosa*, 6vv

29 Metre Jan, *Ave Maria alta stirps*, 5vv

30 [Willaert], *Ave maria ancilla*, 2.p. *Ave Maria fons*, 5vv

31 Adriani Vuillaert, *Ave et gaude [gloriosa Virgo Maria]*, 5vv

*Should be tenor clef

32 Proenestini, *O virgo simul et mater*, 5vv

33 Jo. petr. Proenestini, *Sancta et immaculata*, 2.p. *Benedicta tu*, 6vv

Canon in diatessaron
superius

Feast	Text	Probable Source	Remarks
	Gradual at Mass, Feasts of the B.V.M. (L.U. 1264)	Portinaro 1568, p. 10	
		Gardane 1549[6], p. 3	
Visitation of the B.V.M. (2 July)	Song of Songs 2:13b–14 (Chapter at Nones)	Corvus 1555, p. 1	
	Responsory (L.R. 255)	Gardane 1549[6], p. 18	
	Antiphon, Sunday at Compline (L.U. 274)	Zarlino 1549, p. 6	
Annunciation of the B.V.M. (25 March)	Third responsory at Matins (without versus) (Proc. Mon. 245)	Gardane 1549[6], p. 8	
	Rhymed poem (A.H. 19, 22)	Gardane 1542[10], p. 44	Mod. ed. Willaert OO 4, p. 117.
	Chev. 1871	Jachet 1540, p. 23 (= Jachet)	
		Moderne 1532[9], p. 50, or Willaert 1539 or 1550, no. 22	Mod. ed. Willaert OO 3, p. 114.
		Palestrina 1572, no. 1	Concordance in Bologna Q 27, f. 51. Attributed to Simon Ferrariensis in Schoeffer 1539[8], no. 16; anon. in Piacenza, f. 37. See also no. 82. Mod. ed. Palestrina *Opere* 7, p. 1.
Nativity of Our Lord (25 December)	Sixth Responsory at Matins (L.U. 384)	Palestrina 1572, no. 22	Mod. ed. Palestrina *Opere* 7, p. 146.

34 Gjacheti de Berquem, *Gaude et laetare*, 5vv

35 Adriani Vuillert, *Sub tuum presidium*, 5vv

36 Adriani willaert, *Alma Redemptoris*, 2.p. *Tu quae genuisti*, 6vv

Canon: Fuga trium
temporum in diapente
inferius tam in prima
quam in secunda parte

37 Adriani willaert, *Benedicta es [coelorum Regina]*, 2.p. *Per illud ave*, 7vv

Canon: Fuga trium temporum
in diapente et octo temporum
in diapason

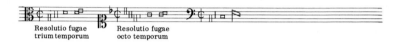

Resolutio fugae   Resolutio fugae
trium temporum   octo temporum

38 Adriani vuillaert, *Inviolata [integra et casta es]*, 2.p. *Tua per precata*, 7vv

Canon: Fuga quatuor temporum in diatessaron   Resolutio fugae
remissum et Fuga septem temporum in diapason   quatuor temporum
remissum   in diatessaron
                                                    remissum et est
                                                    Septima vox

Resolutio fugae septem
temporum in diapason
remissum et est quinta vox

39 Adriani vuillaert, *Salve sancta parens*, 2.p. *Virgo Dei genitrix*, 6vv

Canon: Fuga trium temporum in   Fuga trium temporum in
diapente inferius, et erit sexta vox.   diapente et erit vox tenoris.
Post novem pausas statim incipe   Post vigintiquinque pausas
pro sexta vox   incipe in diapente inferius
                                             pro Tenore

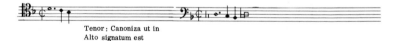

Tenor: Canoniza ut in
Alto signatum est

Feast	Text	Probable Source	Remarks
	Antiphon to the Nunc Dimittis at Compline, Office of the B.V.M. (L.U. 1861)	Willaert 1559, no. 7	Mod. ed. Willaert OO 5, p. 62.
	Antiphon, Sunday at Compline (L.U. 273)	Willaert 1559, no. 13	Mod. ed. Willaert OO 5, p. 109.
	Sequence	Willaert 1559, no. 25	Mod. ed. Willaert OO 5, p. 238.
	Sequence (L.U. 1861)	Willaert 1559, no. 24	Mod. ed. Willaert OO 5, p. 223.
	Introit and verse of the Gradual at Mass (L.U. 1263, 1265)	Willaert 1559, no. 15	Mod. ed. Willaert OO 5, p. 127.

40 Adriani vuillaert, *Praeter rerum ordinem*, 2.p. *Virtus sancti spiritus*, 7vv

Canon. Trinitas in unitate
Fuga. Primo in diatessaron et
diapente. Secundo in diapente
et diatessaron ut signatum est.
Resolutiones fugae predictę
habentur in libro Bassi

Resolutio primę   Resolutio primę
partis fugae in   partis fugae in
diatessaron ex   diapente ex Tenore
Tenore

41 Francisci portinarii, *Regina coeli*, 7vv

Altus secundus et
est sexta vox

Bassus secundus
et est septima vox

42 Gomberth, *Conceptio tua [Dei Genitrix]*, 5vv

43 Continus, *Hodie beata virgo [Maria puerum]*, 5vv

Feast	Text	Probable Source	Remarks
Nativity of Our Lord (25 December)	Sequence (A.H. 20, no. 53)	Willaert 1559, no. 23	Mod. ed. Willaert OO 5, p. 209.
	Antiphon, Sunday at Compline (L.U. 275)	Portinaro 1548, p. 29	
Immaculate Conception of the B.V.M. (8 December)		Gombert 1541 or 1550, p. 28	Mod. ed. Gombert OO 8, p. 59.
Purification of the B.V.M. (2 February)	Antiphon to the Magnificat, 2nd Vespers (L.U. 1367)	Continus 1560/2, p. 6	

Manuscript 30
Inventory derived from the card catalogue of Giovanni D'Alessi in the Biblioteca Capitolare, Treviso

[0]   Benedicti Menchini pistoiensis, *Gabriel angelus*, 2.p. *Michael archangelus*, 5vv

1   H. Scaffen, *Christi corpus ave*, 2.p. *Christi sanguis ave*, 5vv

2   Morales, *Cum natus esset Jesus*, 2.p. *At illi dixerunt*, 3.p. *Et ecce stella*, 5vv

3   Adrian W(illaert), *Laetare sancta mater ecclesia*, 2.p. *Augustine lux doctorum*, 5vv

4   Archadelt, *Signum salutis*, 2.p. *Lapidem quem reprovaverunt*, 5vv

5   Franciscus Patav(inus) [Santacroce], *Magnum mysterium*, 5vv

6   Jachet, *Sufficiebat nobis paupertas*, 2.p. *Heu me fili mi*, 5vv

Mon souvenir
my fayt mourir

7   Giuston, *Ingressus est Raphael*, 5vv

8   Ciprianus Rore, *Pater noster*, 5vv

9   Franc(iscus) Patav(inus) [Santacroce], *Domine Deus omnipotens*, 5vv

10   Francis(cus) Pata(vinus) [Santacroce], *Dirigere et sanctificare*, 5vv

Text[1]	Concordances	Remarks
Insufficient text to determine source		A later addition. D'Alessi: 'Questo mottetto sta scritto nella prima carta dell' Altus, Quintus, Tenor e Bassus e nella prima e terza del Cantus in scrittura minutissima negli spazi lasciati vuoti del mottetto N. 1'.
Chev. 3050		
Gospel at Epiphany (L.U. 461)	Bologna SP 39, f. 51v (anon.); C.S. 13, f. 172v; Treviso 29, no. 3; Scotto 1541[3], no. 13; Rhau 1545[5], p. 100; Montanus & Neuber 1554[10], no. 18	Mod. ed. Morales OO 2, p. 79.
Motet for feast of St Augustine, 28 August	Modena C 313, p. 115; Treviso 4, no. 13; Treviso 36, f. 14; Schoeffer 1539[8], no. 21; Willaert 1539 or 1550, no. 8	Mod. ed. Willaert OO 3, p. 40.
1.p. similar to antiphon (Proc. Mon. 108); 2.p. Ps. 117:22 and antiphon Bene fundata est (L.U. 1247)	See Treviso 29, no. 8.	Attributed to Crecquillon in other sources; see MS 29, no. 8.
Second antiphon, second Nocturn, Octave of Epiphany (V.P. 96)	Treviso 29, no. 1	
Responsory, 3rd Sunday in October (Worc. Ant. 176)	Bologna Q 19, f. 32v	D'Alessi: 'Il Tenor ha due segni di misura e il testo: Mon souvenir my fayt mourir'.
Antiphon, Feast of St Raphael, Archangel, 24 October (Proc. Mon. 199)		
Lord's Prayer	Munich B, f. 66v	Mod. ed. Rore OO 6, p. 49.
Prayer at Prime (L.U. 232)		See transcription below, Appendix, no. 3.
Prayer at Prime (L.U. 233)		

[1] For those motets that are unique to Treviso 30, the identification of the text is conjectural. In several cases the incipits are common to a number of sources.

11 Cuglias, *Ne derelinquas me Domine*, 5vv

12 Metre Jan, *Clementissime Deus*, 2.p. *Tuque sacer Hieronime*, 5vv

13 Morales, *Antoni pater inclite*, 5vv

14 Lupus, *Jam non dicam vos servos*, 2.p. *Cum venerit ille spiritus*, 5vv

15 Ciprianus Rore, *Si resurrexistis una cum Ch(risto)*, 5vv

16 Innocentius Alberti, *Non est in hominis potestate*, 2.p. *Non enim delectaris*, 5vv

17 Guglielmus Testoris, *Domine ante te*, 5vv

18 Metallo, *Immensis beneficiis Hieronymum*, 5vv

[19] [Willaert], *Peccata mea*, 6vv

Second series

1 Franc(esco) Portina(ro), *Quis tuus has nostras*, 6vv

2 Franc(esco) Portinaro, *Eripe me domine*, 7vv

Canon. post semibrevem,
me statim sequere in
dyatessaron superius

Text	Concordances	Remarks
Ps. 37:22 or antiphon, Friday at Vespers (L.U. 302)		
Motet for Feast of St Jerome, 30 September	Treviso 29, no. 55	
First strophe of hymn 'de S. Antonio Thebano' (Chev. 1203), Feast of St Anthony, Abbot, 17 January	Treviso 29, no. 5	D'Alessi: 'Il nome dell'Autore è stato aggiunto da mano posteriore'.
1.p. Responsory (without versus) (L.U. 1847); 2.p. cf. John 16:13	See Kabis, 1, 39–40	Mod. ed. Kabis, 2, pp. 114–23. Attributed to Richafort in most other sources.
Probably Tobias 3:20–3		
Insufficient text to determine source; possibly contemporary	Treviso 29, no. 29	D'Alessi: 'In fine alla parte del Bassus sta scritto: "Ad clarissimum Jo. Baptistam Contarenum patavii praetorem dignissimum Guglielmus Textoris carceratus"'.
Motet for Feast of St Jerome, 30 September		
Responsory (Lucca Ant. 84)	Modena C 314, p. 86; Regensburg AR 893, no. 36; Willaert 1559, no. 14	Mod. ed. Willaert OO 5, p. 119.
Contemporary		D'Alessi: 'Mottetto in onore di Enrico Brunesvic'.
Ps. 139:1–5	Portinaro 1568, p. 25	

3 Franc(esco) Portinaro, *Benedicta et venerabilis*, 6vv

4 Franc(esco) Portenaro, *Domine ne in furore*, 2.p. *[Convertere, Domine] Et eripe animam meam*, 6vv

5 Jo. Nasco, *Memor esto*, 2.p. *Haec me consolata est*, 6vv

In subdyatessaron

6 *Cantate cęli domino*, 6vv

Canon in dyapente

7 Adriani W(illaert), *Infelix ego*, 2.p. *Ad te igitur*, 6vv

8 Adriani W(illaert), *Enixa est puerpera*, 2.p. *Parvoque lacte*, 6vv

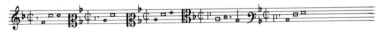

9 Joannes Continus, *Miseremini mei*, 2.p. *Scio enim quod*, 6vv

10 Ghislinus Danchera, *Suscipe Verbum*, 2.p. *Paries quidem filium*, 6vv

Resolutio

11 *Sancte Marce*, 2.p. *O gemma clara martirum*, 6vv

12 *Apparens Christus*, 2.p. *Non relinquam vos orphanos*, 6vv

13 M. Jan, *O felix custos martirum*, 2.p. *Rogamus te ergo*, 6vv

Resolutio

Text	Concordances	Remarks
Gradual at Mass, Feasts of the B.V.M. (L.U. 1264)	Treviso 29, no. II/22; Portinaro 1568, p. 10	
Ps. 6:1–7	Portinaro 1568, p. 1	
Ps. 118:49–50		Second soprano in canon at the lower fourth. Transcription of 1.p. below, Appendix, no. 5.
		Tenor in canon at the fifth.
Opening paragraph of Savonarola's meditation on Psalm 50; see Macey, pp. 425–6.	Edinburgh 64, f. 121v (anon.); Modena C 314, p. 92; Regensburg AR 893, no. 38; Wolfenbüttel 293, no. 37; Montanus & Neuber [1556][9], no. 34	
The lines of the hymn (Stäblein, p. 31) are separated by refrain-like tropes: 'fulget dies', 'fulget dies ista diei solemnia' and 'fulget dies ista diei solemnia celebrat ecclesia'.	C.S. 46, fol. 42v; Kriesstein 1540[7], no. 5 (1.p. only)	
Job 19:21–2, 23b–27. Lesson VIII at Matins (beginning with Job 19:20), Office of the Dead (L.U. 1797)	Modena C 314, p. 8	
Responsory, Feasts of the B.V.M. (Proc. Mon. 245)		C.f. *Ave Maria*. Transcription below, Appendix, no. 1.

14   Vincen(tius) Ruffus, *Deus in nomine tuo*, 2.p. *Averte mala*, 6vv

15   M. Jan, *Tua est potentia*, 6vv

vocales docent cantum,
quod lilia florent

16   Matthias (Werrecorre), *Congregati sunt inimici*, 6vv

17   Jachet, *Missa Surge Petre*, 6vv

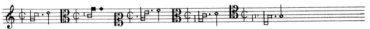

18   Franc(esco) Portina(ro), *Missa Surge Petre*, 6vv

19   Jousquin, *Benedicta es celorum regina*, 2.p. *Per illud ave*, 3.p. *Nunc mater exora*, 6vv

20   Noe balduin, *Tu Domine universorum*, 6vv

Text	Concordances	Remarks
Ps. 53	Ruffo 1555, no. 7	
Antiphon to the Magnificat, Saturday before the 5th Sunday of October (L.U. 995)	Kriesstein 1540[7], no. 2 (= Danckerts)	C.f. *Da pacem*. D'Alessi: 'Canone enigmatico: Il quintus porta uno stemma e sotto la scritta: "Vocales docent cantum, quod lilia florent"'. The 'stemma', sketched by D'Alessi, is the coat of arms of Paul III surmounted by a papal tiara and keys.
Responsory (without versus), Sunday in October (Worc. Ant. 181)	Treviso 4, no. 72 (Ruer); Kriesstein 1540[7], no. 1	C.f. *Da pacem*.
	Jachet 1557	Based on his own motet.
	Munich 45, f. 1	Based on Jachet's motet.
Sequence for the Annunciation	See Smijers, pp. X–XIII	Mod. ed. Smijers, p. 11.
Prayer for the well-being of the soul; see Sparks, p. 13	Kriesstein 1545[3], no. 2 (with 2.p. Da pacem)	Tenor in canon at the unison (in Treviso, erroneously resolved at upper octave).

1. Suscipe verbum Virgo Maria

Ghislinus Danchera
Treviso 30, second series, no. 10

* Reconstructed to bar 52 in both *partes*
1. Changed to 'Virgo Maria' in a later hand
2. Changed to 'Virgo' in a later hand

115

3. Orig.: C

4. Orig.: rest missing

119

5. Orig.: semper intacta

6. Orig.: F

2.   Deus alma spes

Petrus Antonius Spalenza
Treviso 29, no. 71

3. Domine Deus omnipotens

Franc(iscus) Pat(avinus)
[Santacroce]
Treviso 30, no. 9

129

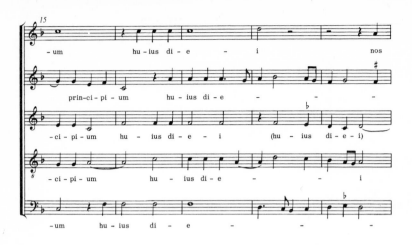

1. Orig.: dot missing

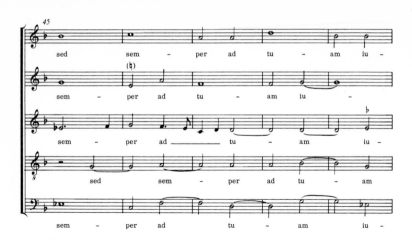

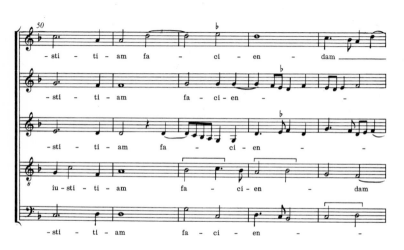

133

4. Inviolata integra et casta es

Jo. Nasco
Treviso 29, second series, no. 1

SECUNDA PARS

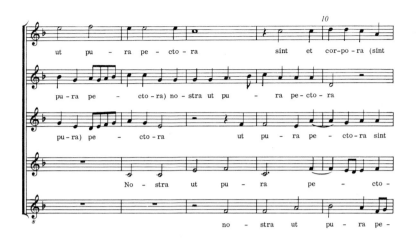

141

5. Memor esto

Jo. Nasco
Treviso 30, second series, no. 5

1. The bracketed notes replace a breve and semibreve pause.

Index of Composers

All compositions are in Treviso 29 unless marked 'Tr 30'. Contrafactum texts are given in italics.

Anonymous
Apparens Christus, Tr 30, no. II/12
Ave Confessor gloriose Liberalis; see Verdelot
Ave Maria ancilla; *see* Willaert
Ave sanctissima Maria Mater Dei, II/23
Beati evangeliste Mathei; see Contino
Cantate caeli Domino, Tr 30, no. II/6
Deus qui nos; see Contino
Felix nanque es, II/25
Gaude et laetare; see Contino
Gaudeamus; see Willaert
Misit rex incredulus; see Comes
O praesul venerabilis; see Jachet
Omnipotens sempiterne Deus; see Contino
Sancte Marce, Tr 30, no. II/11
Sicut lilium, II/9
Suscipe verbum Virgo Maria, II/27
Veni Sponsa Christi, 124
Virgo Maria speciosissima, II/13
Virtute magna reddebant, 103

Alberti, Innocenzo
Hic est dies egregius, 23
Non est in hominis potestate, Tr 30, no. 16

Animuccia, Giovanni
Fuit homo missus, 35

Arcadelt, Jacques
Diem festum sacratissime, 8
Signum salutis; *see* 8 and Tr 30, no. 4

Arnoldo (Caussin?)
Rosa de spinis, II/18

Bauldeweyn, Noel
Tu Domine universorum, Tr 30, no. II/20

Berchem, Jachet
Gaude et laetare, II/34
In illo tempore dixit Jesus, 25
Qualis es dilecta mea, II/3

Cambio, Perissone
Ad te Domine animam meam; *see* 75

Ave ignea columna, 75

Comes, Bartolomeo
Assumpsit Jesus Petrum, 47
Ave martir egregie, 12
Cum iocunditate; *see* 53 and II/15
Domine ne longe facias; *see* 14
Domus mea domus orationis, 125
Gaudent in coelis anime sanctorum, 110
Misit rex incredulus, 53
O martir egregie; *see* Ave martir egregie
Te gloriosus apostolorum, 61
Virgo martir, 14

Contino, Giovanni
Assumpta est Maria; *see* 54
Austriae stirpis; *see* 60
Ave vivens hostia; *see* 94
Beati evangeliste Mathei, 54
Benedictus qui venit, 85
Deus cuius dextera, 40
Deus qui beatum, 94
Deus qui nobis sub sacramento; *see* 40
Deus qui nos, 60
Gaude et laetare, 66
Hic est praecursor dilectus, 36
Hodie beata Virgo Maria puerum, II/43
Hodie Christus natus est, 80
Innocentes pro Christo, 83
Intervenientibus Domine, 42
Iste est qui ante Deum, 118
Iste sanctus pro lege Dei, 105
Laetentur coeli, *see* 85
Laudemus Dominum, 98
Maria stabat ad monumentum; *see* 78
Miseremini mei, Tr 30, no. II/9
O admirabile commercium; *see* 42
O beatum virum, 68
O magnum mysterium; *see* 51
O quam gloriosum est regnum, 65
O quam magnificum, 49
O stupor et gaudium; *see* 118
Omnipotens sempiterne Deus, 51
Patefactae sunt ianuae, 81
Prudens et vigilans, 72
Quia vidisti me Thoma, 78

145

Sacerdos et pontifex, 112
Sancti Dei omnes, 63
Sanctorum martyrum tuorum; see 112
Surge Petre et indue te; see 98
Tempus est ut revertar; see 81
Texebat viridem cloris; see 49 and 66
Ut te muneribus; see 105

Corvo, Giovanni Battista
Hodie beata Virgo Maria puerum, 11
Nos autem gloriari oportet, 26
Surge propera amica mea, II/24

Crecquillon, Thomas
Signum salutis; see 8 and Tr 30, n. 4

Cuglias
Ne derelinquas me Domine, Tr 30, no. 11

Danckerts, Ghiselin
Suscipe verbum Virgo Maria, Tr 30, no. II/10
Tu es vas electionis, 9
Tua est potentia, Tr 30, no. II/15

Finot. See Phinot.

Gallicus. See Comes.

Garugli, Bernardino
Dum sacrum misterium, 30
Gaudent in caelis, 31
Vocatus Joseph, 97

Gislinus. See Danckerts.

Giuston
Ingressus est Raphael, Tr 30, no. 7

Gombert, Nicolas
Caeciliam cantate; see 113
Conceptio tua Dei Genitrix, II/42
Egregie martir Sebastiane, 7
Gabriel nunciavit Mariae; see 19
In tua pacientia, 77
Juravit Dominus, 113
O felix Anna, 45
Sancte Gregori, 16
Surge Petre et indue te, 37
Suscipe verbum Virgo Maria, 18
Tu es Petrus, 15
Veni dilecta mea; see 77
Veni electa mea, 122
Venite ad me omnes, 101

Jachet of Mantua
Alma Redemptoris Mater, II/17
Ave Maria alta stirps; see II/29
Ave quam colunt angeli, II/7
Ave Virgo gratiosa, II/28
Descendi in hortum, II/2
Enceladi ceique soror; see 90
Missa Surge Petre, Tr 30, no. II/17
Murus tuus dilecta, II/11

O felix custos, 17
O lampas ardens, 6
O praesul venerabilis, 67
O quam praeclara sunt; see 17 and 67
Repleatur os meum; see 117
Similabo eum, 117
Stans beata Agnes, 90
Sufficiebat nobis paupertas, Tr 30, no. 6

Jhan, Maitre
Ambulans Jesus iuxta mare, 73
Ave Maria alta stirps, II/29
Clementissime Deus, 55 and Tr 30, no. 12
Da ecclesiae tuae, 34
O felix custos martirum, Tr 30, no. II/13
Praesul sanctissime Augustine, 52
Sacrae legis Christianae, 58
Sancte Jacobe apostole, 44
Tua est potentia, Tr 30, no. II/15

Josquin des Prez
Benedicta es coelorum Regina, Tr 30, no. II/19

Lafage, Johannes
Partus et integritas; see 39
Sancte Paule apostole, 39

Lasso, Orlando di
Antoni pater inclite, 87
Confitemini Domino; see 106
Elegit te Dominus, 93
Illustra faciem tuam; see 93
Non vos me elegistis, 102
O lux Italiae, 95
Qui vult venire, 106
Surrexit pastor bonus; see 87
Veni in hortum meum; see 95
Videntes stellam Magi, 86

Lupi, Johannes
Isti sunt viri sancti; see 16
Sancte Marce evangelista, 20
Vidi speciosam; see 20

Lupus
Jam non dicam vos servos, Tr 30, no. 14

Menchini, Benedetto
Gabriel angelus, Tr 30, no. [0]

Metallo, Grammatio
Immensis beneficiis Hieronymum, Tr 30, no. 18

Morales, Cristóbal de
Antoni pater inclite, 5 and Tr 30, no. 13
Cum natus esset, 3 and Tr 30, no. 2
Tu es Petrus; see 15

Moreau, Simon
Tu es Petrus; see 15

Nasco, Giovanni
Inviolata integra et casta es, II/1
Magnificemus Deum salvatorem, 92
Memor esto, Tr 30, no. II/5

Palestrina, Angelo
Circuire possum Domine, 27

Palestrina, Giovanni Pierluigi da
Angelus Domini descendit; see 107
Beatus Dei famulus, 70
Canite tuba in Sion; see 111
Columna es immobilis, 76
Congrega, Domine; see 131
Corona aurea super caput eius, 104
Filiae Jerusalem venite et videte, 107
Fuit homo missus, 129
Gaude Barbara; see 70
Haec est vera fraternitas, 111
In medio ecclesiae, 82
Inclitae sanctae virginis Catherinae, 128
O lux et decus Hispaniae, 130
O quam metuendus, 127
O sancte praesul Nicolae, 74
O Virgo simul et Mater, II/32; see also 82
Omnipotens sempiterne Deus, 132
Peccantem me quotidie; see 84
Praeceptor bonum est, 131
Sancta et immaculata, II/33
Sanctificavit Dominus tabernaculum, 126
Silvester beatissimus, 84
Tradent enim vos, 100
Tu es Petrus, 38

Patavino, Francesco. See Santacroce, Francesco.

Perissone. See Cambio.

Phinot, Dominicus
Agatha laetissime, 13
Auribus percipe Domine; see 13
Descendit Spiritus Sanctus, 4
Gabriel nunciavit Mariae, 19
Illuminare Hierusalem; see 2
Istorum est enim regnum, 108
O quam gloriosum est regnum, 62
Osculetur me osculo oris sui, II/19
Surge illuminare Jerusalem, 2
Tanto tempore vobiscum sum, 24; see also 4
Te gloriosus apostolorum, 64
Tua est potentia; see 9

Portinaro, Francesco
Absterget Deus omnem lachrymam, 109
Benedicta et venerabilis, II/22 and Tr 30, II/3
Da pacem; see 115
Domine ne in furore, Tr 30, no. II/4
Dum esset summus pontifex, 115
Eripe me Domine, Tr 30, no. II/2

Laudemus Deum, 91
Missa Surge Petre, Tr 30, no. II/18
Quis tuus has nostras, Tr 30, no. II/1
Regina coeli, II/41
Sancta et immaculata; see 91
Sicut cedrus exaltata sum, II/21
Vidi speciosam sicut columbam, II/5

Richafort, Johannes
Jam non dicam vos servos; see Tr 30, no. 14
Veni Sponsa Christi, 120

Rore, Cipriano de
Angustiae mihi; see 119
Cantantibus organis; see 96
Domine quis habitabit; see 43
Exaudiat me Dominus; see 121
Gaude Maria Virgo cunctas haereses, II/4
Hic vir despiciens mundum, 119
Hodie scietis, 79
In Domino confido; see 88
Mulier quae erat, 43
O Gregori, 96
Pater noster, Tr 30, no. 8
Petre amas me, 88
Prudentes virgines aptate lampades, 121
Pulchrior italicis; see 79
Regnum mundi, 123
Si ignoras te, II/12
Si resurrexistis una cum Christo, Tr 30, no. 15
Usquequo Domine; see 123
Virtute magna reddebant; see 103

Ruffo, Vincenzo
Deus in nomine tuo, Tr 30, no. II/14

Santacroce, Francesco (Francesco Patavino)
Dirigere et sanctificare, Tr 30, no. 10
Domine Deus omnipotens, Tr 30, no. 9
Magnum misterium, 1 and Tr 30, no. 5

Scaffen, Henricus
Christi corpus ave, Tr 30, no. 1
Senex puerum portabat, 10

Simon Ferrariensis
Ave et gaude gloriosa Virgo Maria; see II/31

Spalenza, Pietro Antonio
Deus alma spes, 71

Testore, Guglielmo
Domine ante te; see 29 and Tr 30, no. 17
In ferventis olei, 29

Tugdual
Gloriosum diem, 28

Verdelot, Philippe
Ave confessor gloriose Liberalis, 22
In te Domine speravi; *see* 22

Werrecorre, Matthias
Congregati sunt inimici, Tr 30, no. II/16

Willaert, Adrian
Alma Redemptoris Mater, II/36
Ave et gaude gloriosa Virgo Maria, II/31
Ave Maria ancilla, II/30
Ave Virgo sponsa Dei, II/14
Beata viscera Mariae, II/8
Beatus Bernardus, 50
Beatus Laurentius orabat dicens, 48
Benedicta es coelorum Regina, II/37
Benedictus Redemptor omnium, 46
Christi martir sancte Chiliane; see O Christi martir
Creator omnium Deus; *see* 116
Domine Jesu Christe fili Dei; *see* 50
Enixa est puerpera, Tr 30, no. II/8
Gaudeamus, 57
Gaudeamus omnes, 59
Infelix ego, Tr 30, no. II/7
Inviolata integra et casta es, II/38
Laetare sancta mater ecclesia, Tr 30, no. 3

Miserere nostri Deus; *see* 32 and 59
O beatum pontificem, 69
O Christi martir sancte Chiliane, 41
O doctor optime, 116
O gloriosa Domina, II/6
O proles Hispaniae, 33
O sodales Sancti Vindemialis et Florentii, 32
Peccata mea, Tr 30, no. 19
Più volte già dal bel sembiante; *see* 41
Praeter rerum ordinem, II/40
Quando fra l'altre donne; *see* 57
Salve sancta parens, II/39
Sancte Francisce propere, 56
Sub tuum praesidium, II/35

Zarlino, Gioseffo
Adiuro vos, II/20
Amavit eum Dominus, 114
Ave Regina coelorum, II/26
Beatissimus Marcus discipulus, 21
Clodia quem genuit; *see* 99
Ecce tu pulchra es, II/10
Hodie sanctus Benedictus, 99
O beatum pontificem; *see* 114
Sebastianus Dei cultor, 89
Virgo prudentissima, II/16

Index of Compositions

All compositions are in Treviso 29 unless marked 'Tr 30'.

Absterget Deus, 2.p. Non exurient (Portinaro), 109
Ad te Domine animam meam (Perissone Cambio); see 75
Adiuro vos (Zarlino), II/20
Agatha laetissime, 2.p. Nobilissimis orta natalibus (Phinot), 13
Alma Redemptoris Mater, 2.p. Tu quae genuisti (Jachet), II/17; (Willaert), II/36
Amavit eum Dominus (Zarlino), 114
Ambulans Jesus iuxta mare, 2.p. At illi continuo (Maitre Jhan), 73
Angelus Domini descendit (Palestrina); see 107
Angustiae mihi (Rore); see 119
Antoni pater inclite (Lasso), 87; (Morales), 5 and Tr 30, no. 13
Apparens Christus, 2.p. Non relinquam vos orphanos (Anon.), Tr 30, no. II/12
Assumpsit Jesus Petrum et Jacobum et Joannem (Comes), 47
Assumpta est Maria (Contino); see 54
Auribus percipe Domine (Phinot); see 13
Austriae stirpis (Contino); see 60
Ave Confessor gloriose Liberalis (Verdelot), 22
Ave et gaude gloriosa Virgo Maria (Willaert or Simon Ferrariensis), II/31
Ave ignea columna, 2.p. O Dei electe (Perissone Cambio), 75
Ave Maria alta stirps (Maitre Jhan or Jachet), II/29
Ave Maria ancilla, 2.p. Ave Maria fons (Willaert), II/30
Ave martir egregie o salutaris medice (Comes), 12
Ave quam colunt angeli, 2.p. Audi quid (Jachet), II/7
Ave Regina coelorum (Zarlino), II/26
Ave sanctissima Maria Mater Dei (Anon.), II/23
Ave Virgo gratiosa (Jachet), II/28
Ave Virgo sponsa Dei, 2.p. Igitur nos merito (Willaert), II/14
Ave vivens hostia (Contino); see 94

Beata viscera Mariae Virginis (Willaert), II/8
Beati evangeliste Mathei (Contino), 54
Beatissimus Marcus discipulus, 2.p. Accepto evangelio (Zarlino), 21
Beatus Bernardus (Willaert), 50
Beatus Dei famulus, 2.p. Gaude Tarvisina civitas (Palestrina), 70
Beatus Laurentius orabat dicens (Willaert), 48
Benedicta es coelorum Regina, 2.p. Per illud ave (Josquin), Tr 30, no. II/19; (Willaert), II/37
Benedicta et venerabilis es (Portinaro), II/22 and Tr 30, no. II/3
Benedictus qui venit (Contino), 85
Benedictus Redemptor omnium, 2.p. Magne pater sancte Dominice (Willaert), 46

Caeciliam cantate (Gombert); see 113
Canite tuba in Sion (Palestrina); see 111
Cantantibus organis (Rore); see 96
Cantate caeli Domino (Anon.), Tr 30, no. II/6
Christi corpus ave, 2.p. Christi sanguis ave (Scaffen), Tr 30, no. 1
Christi martir Sancte Chiliane; see O Christi martir

149

Circuire possum Domine, 2.p. In hac cruce (Angelo Palestrina), 27
Clementissime Deus, 2.p. Tuque sacer Hieronime (Maitre Jhan), 55 and Tr 30, no. 12
Clodia quem genuit (Zarlino); see 99
Columna es immobilis (Palestrina), 76
Conceptio tua Dei Genitrix (Gombert), II/42
Confitemini Domino (Lasso); see 106
Congrega, Domine (Palestrina); see 131
Congregati sunt inimici (Werrecorre), Tr 30, no. II/16
Corona aurea, 2.p. Domine praevenisti (Palestrina), 104
Creator omnium Deus (Willaert); see 116
Cum iucunditate, 2.p. Corde et animo (Comes), II/15; see also 53
Cum natus esset, 2.p. At illi, 3.p. Et ecce stella (Morales), 3 and Tr 30, no. 2

Da ecclesiae tuae (Maitre Jhan), 34
Da pacem (Portinaro); see 115
Descendi in hortum (Jachet), II/2
Descendit Spiritus Sanctus (Phinot), 4
Deus alma spes (Spalenza), 71
Deus cuius dextera (Contino), 40
Deus in nomine tuo, 2.p. Averte mala (Ruffo), Tr 30, no. II/14
Deus qui beatum (Contino), 94
Deus qui nobis sub sacramento (Contino); see 40
Deus qui nos (Contino), 60
Diem festum sacratissime, 2.p. Dexteram eius (Arcadelt), 8
Dirigere et sanctificare (Santacroce), Tr 30, no. 10
Domine ante te (Testore); see 29 and Tr 30, no. 17
Domine Deus omnipotens (Santacroce), Tr 30, no. 9
Domine Jesu Christe fili Dei (Willaert); see 50
Domine ne in furore, 2.p. Et eripe animam meam (Portinaro), Tr 30, no. II/4
Domine ne longe facias (Comes); see 14
Domine quis habitabit (Rore); see 43
Domus mea domus orationis, 2.p. Petite et accipietis (Comes), 125
Dum esset summus pontifex (Portinaro), 115
Dum sacrum misterium (Garugli), 30

Ecce tu pulchra es amica mea (Zarlino), II/10
Egregie martir Sebastiane, 2.p. Socius enim (Gombert), 7
Elegit te Dominus, 2.p. Imola Deo (Lasso), 93
Enceladi ceique soror (Jachet); see 90
Enixa est puerpera, 2.p. Parvoque lacte (Willaert), Tr 30, no. II/8
Eripe me Domine (Portinaro), Tr 30, no. II/2
Exaudiat me Dominus (Rore); see 121

Felix nanque es, 2.p. Ora pro populo (Anon.), II/25
Filiae Jerusalem venite et videte, 2.p. Quoniam confortavit (Palestrina), 107
Fuit homo missus, 2.p. Erat Joannes (Palestrina), 129
Fuit homo missus a Deo (Animuccia), 35

Gabriel angelus, 2.p. Michael arcangelus (Menchini), Tr 30, no. [0]
Gabriel nunciavit Mariae, 2.p. Pneumatis latet (Phinot or Gombert), 19
Gaude Barbara (Palestrina); see 70
Gaude et laetare (Berchem), II/34
Gaude et laetare, 2.p. Gaude igitur Tarvisina civitas (Contino), 66
Gaude Maria Virgo cunctas haereses, 2.p. Gabrielem Archangelum (Rore), II/4
Gaudeamus, 2.p. Cantemus [Willaert], 57
Gaudeamus omnes (Willaert), 59
Gaudent in coelis (Comes), 110; (Garugli), 31
Gloriosum diem, 2.p. Trophaeum crucis (Tugdual), 28

Haec est vera fraternitas, 2.p. Ecce quam bonum (Palestrina), 111
Hic est dies egregius sanctissimi Liberalis, 2.p. Hodie beatum (Alberti), 23
Hic est praecursor dilectus (Contino), 36
Hic vir despiciens mundum (Rore), 119
Hodie beata Virgo Maria puerum (Contino), II/43; (Corvo), 11

Hodie Christus natus est (Contino), 80
Hodie sanctus Benedictus (Zarlino), 99
Hodie scietis (Rore), 79

Illuminare Jerusalem (Phinot); see Surge illuminare Jerusalem
Illustra faciem tuam (Lasso); see 93
Immensis beneficiis Hieronymum (Metallo), Tr 30, no. 18
In Domino confido (Rore); see 88
In ferventis olei (Testore), 29
In illo tempore dixit Jesus, 2.p. Domine ostende nobis (Berchem), 25
In medio ecclesiae, 2.p. Iucunditatem et exultationem (Palestrina), 82
In te Domine speravi (Verdelot); see 22
In tua pacientia, 2.p. Lucia virgo (Gombert), 77
Inclitae sanctae virginis (Palestrina), 128
Infelix ego, 2.p. Ad te igitur (Willaert) Tr 30, no. II/7
Ingressus est Raphael (Giuston), Tr 30, no. 7
Innocentes pro Christo (Contino), 83
Intervenientibus Domine (Contino), 42
Inviolata, 2.p. Nostra ut pura (Nasco), II/1
Inviolata, 2.p. Tua per precata (Willaert), II/38
Iste est qui ante Deum, 2.p. Iste est qui contempsit (Contino), 118
Iste Sanctus pro lege Dei (Contino), 105
Isti sunt viri sancti (Lupi); see 16
Istorum est enim regnum (Phinot), 108

Jam non dicam vos servos, 2.p. Cum venerit ille spiritus (Richafort), Tr 30, no. 14
Juravit Dominus et non paenitebit, 2.p. Dixit Dominus (Gombert), 113

Laetare sancta mater ecclesia, 2.p. Augustine lux doctorum (Willaert), Tr 30, no. 3
Laetentur caeli (Contino); see 85
Laudemus Deum, 2.p. Hic est vas (Portinaro), 91
Laudemus Dominum, 2.p. Benedictum sit (Contino), 98

Magnificemus Deum salvatorem (Nasco), 92
Magnum misterium (Santacroce), 1 and Tr 30, no. 5
Maria stabat ad monumentum (Contino); see 78
Memor esto, 2.p. Haec me consolata est (Nasco), Tr 30, no. II/5
Miseremini mei, 2.p. Scio enim quod (Contino), Tr 30, no. II/9
Miserere nostri Deus (Willaert); see 32 and 59
Misit rex incredulus, 2.p. Herodes enim (Comes), 53
Missa Surge Petre (Jachet), Tr 30, no. II/17; (Portinaro), Tr 30, no. II/18
Mulier quae erat (Rore), 43
Murus tuus dilecta, 2.p. Ego murus sum (Jachet), II/11

Ne derelinquas me Domine (Cuglias), Tr 30, no. 11
Non est in hominis potestate, 2.p. Non enim delectaris (Alberti), Tr 30, no. 16
Non vos me elegistis (Lasso), 102
Nos autem gloriari oportet (Corvo), 26

O admirabile commercium (Contino); see 42
O beatum pontificem (Willaert), 69; (Zarlino); see 114
O beatum virum (Contino), 68
O Christi martir sancte Chiliane (Willaert), 41
O doctor optime (Willaert), 116
O felix Anna, 2.p. O Anna purissima (Gombert), 45
O felix custos (Jachet), 17
O felix custos martirum, 2.p. Rogamus te ergo (Maitre Jhan), Tr 30, no. II/13
O gloriosa Domina, 2.p. Maria Mater gratiae (Willaert), II/6
O Gregori (Rore), 96
O lampas ardens (Jachet), 6
O lux et decus Hispaniae, 2.p. O singulare praesidium (Palestrina), 130
O lux Italiae (Lasso), 95
O magnum mysterium (Contino); see 51
O martir egregie (Comes); see 12

O praesul venerabilis (Jachet), 67
O proles Hispaniae (Willaert), 33
O quam gloriosum est regnum (Contino), 65; (Phinot), 62
O quam magnificum (Contino), 49
O quam metuendus (Palestrina), 127
O quam praeclara sunt (Jachet); see 17 and 67
O sancte praesul Nicolae, 2.p. Gaude praesul optime (Palestrina), 74
O sodales sancti Vindemialis et Florentii (Willaert), 32
O stupor et gaudium (Contino); see 118
O Virgo simul et Mater, lux maxima mundi (Palestrina), II/32; see also 82
Omnipotens sempiterne Deus (Contino), 51; (Palestrina), 132
Osculetur me osculo oris sui (Phinot), II/19

Partus et integritas (Lafage); see 39
Patefactae sunt ianuae, 2.p. Mortem enim (Contino), 81
Pater noster (Rore), Tr 30, no. 8
Peccantem me quotidie (Palestrina); see 84
Peccata mea (Willaert), Tr 30, no. 19
Petre amas me, 2.p. Simon Joannis (Rore), 88
Più volte già dal bel sembiante (Willaert); see 41
Praeceptor bonum est, 2.p. Non enim sciebat (Palestrina), 131
Praesul sanctissime Augustine (Maitre Jhan), 52
Praeter rerum ordinem, 2.p. Virtus Sancti Spiritus (Willaert), II/40
Prudens et vigilans (Contino), 72
Prudentes virgines aptate lampades (Rore), 121
Pulchrior italicis (Rore); see 79

Qualis es dilecta mea (Berchem), II/3
Quando fra l'altre donne (Willaert); see 57
Qui vult venire (Lasso), 106
Quia vidisti me Thoma, 2.p. Infer digitum (Contino), 78
Quis tuus has nostras (Portinaro), Tr 30, no. II/1

Regina coeli (Portinaro), II/41
Regnum mundi, 2.p. Exultavit cor meum (Rore), 123
Repleatur os meum (Jachet); see 117
Rosa de spinis protulit, 2.p. Miranda salutatio (Arnoldo), II/18

Sacerdos et pontifex (Contino), 112
Sacrae legis Christianae, 2.p. Precamur ergo supplices (Maitre Jhan), 58
Salve sancta parens, 2.p. Virgo Dei Genitrix (Willaert), II/39
Sancta et immaculata, 2.p. Benedicta tu (Palestrina), II/33; (Portinaro); see 91
Sancte Francisce propere (Willaert), 56
Sancte Gregori (Gombert), 16
Sancte Jacobe apostole, 2.p. O lux et decus Hispaniae (Maitre Jhan), 44
Sancte Marce, 2.p. O gemma clara martirum (Anon.), Tr 30, no. II/11
Sancte Marce evangelista (Lupi), 20
Sancte Paule Apostole (Lafage), 39
Sancti Dei omnes (Contino), 63
Sanctificavit Dominus tabernaculum (Palestrina), 126
Sanctorum martyrum tuorum (Contino); see 112
Sebastianus Dei cultor (Zarlino), 89
Senex puerum portabat (Scaffen), 10
Si ignoras te, 2.p. Surge propera amica mea (Rore), II/12
Si resurrexisti una cum Christo (Rore), Tr 30, no. 15
Sicut cedrus exaltata sum, 2.p. In plateis sicut (Portinaro), II/21
Sicut lilium (Anon.), II/9
Signum salutis, 2.p. Lapidem quem reprovaverunt (Arcadelt or Crecquillon); see 8 and
    Tr 30, no. 4
Silvester beatissimus (Palestrina), 84
Similabo eum (Jachet), 117
Stans beata Agnes (Jachet), 90
Sub tuum presidium (Willaert), II/35
Sufficiebat nobis paupertas, 2.p. Heu me fili mi (Jachet), Tr 30, no. 6

Surge illuminare Jerusalem, 2.p. Omnes de Saba (Phinot), 2
Surge Petre et indue te, 2.p. Angelus Domini (Contino); *see* 98; (Gombert), 37
Surge propera amica mea speciosa mea (Corvo), II/24
Surrexit pastor bonus (Lasso); *see* 87
Suscipe verbum, 2.p. Paries quidem (Danckerts), Tr 30, no. II/10; (Gombert), 18
Suscipe verbum Virgo Maria (Anon.), II/27

Tanto tempore vobiscum sum (Phinot), 24; *see also* 4
Te gloriosus apostolorum (Comes), 61; (Phinot), 64
Tempus est ut revertar (Contino); *see* 81
Texebat viridem cloris (Contino); *see* 49 and 66
Tradent enim vos (Palestrina), 100
Tu Domine universorum (Bauldeweyn) Tr 30, no. II/20
Tu es Petrus, 2.p. Quodcumque ligaveris (Gombert, Morales or Moreau), 15; (Palestrina), 38
Tu es vas electionis, 2.p. Intercede pro nobis (Danckerts), 9
Tua est potentia (Maitre Jhan or Danckerts), Tr 30, no. II/15; (Phinot); *see* 9

Usquequo Domine (Rore); *see* 123
Ut te muneribus (Contino); *see* 105

Veni dilecta mea (Gombert); *see* 77
Veni electa mea (Gombert), 122
Veni in hortum meum (Lasso); *see* 95
Veni sponsa Christi (Anon.), 124; (Richafort), 120
Venite ad me omnes qui laboratis (Gombert), 101
Videntes stellam, 2.p. Et apertis thesauris (Lasso), 86
Vidi speciosam sicut columbam (Lupi); *see* 20; (Portinaro), II/5
Virgo Maria speciosissima, 2.p. Virgo Maria virga Jesse (Anon.), II/13
Virgo martir, 2.p. Ora pro nobis (Comes), 14
Virgo prudentissima (Zarlino), II/16
Virtute magna, 2.p. Repleti quidem (Rore?), 103
Vocatus Joseph, 2.p. Introducit Jesus (Garugli), 97

General Index

Aaron, Pietro, 50 n. 3
Absterget Deus omnem lachrymam (Portinaro), 35, 92–3
Accademia Filarmonica, 13
Ad preces nostras (Spalenza), 53
Ad te Domine animam meam (Cambio), 9, 34, 87
Adieu soulas (Danckerts), 40 n. 21
Adiuro vos (Zarlino), 34, 98–9
Agatha laetissime (Phinot), 5, 9, 14, 51, 74–5
Agee, Richard, 38 nn. 12–13
Alberti, Innocenzo, 4–5, 36–7, 45, 76–7, 108–9
Albrecht, Hans, 7
Alexandria, 10 n. 15
All Saints, 18, 22 n. 10, 25, 83, 85
Alma Redemptoris Mater (Jachet), 98–9
Alma Redemptoris Mater (Willaert), 35, 44, 102–3
Amavit eum Dominus (Zarlino), 7, 9, 14, 92–3
Ambulans Jesus iuxta mare (Maitre Jhan), 36, 84–5
Anerio, Giovanni Francesco, 20–1, 23–4
Angelus Domini descendit (Palestrina), 9, 14, 34, 93
Anglés, Higinio, 70
Angustiae mihi (Rore), 9, 14, 34, 95
Animuccia, Giovanni, 4, 21 n. 10, 67, 78–9
Annunciation of the B.V.M., 10, 16, 75, 97, 101, 113
Antoni pater inclite (Lasso), 6, 9, 88–9
Antoni pater inclite (Morales), 37–8, 72–3, 108–9
Antwerp, 23
Apparens Christus (Anon.), 110–11
Aquileia, 8 n. 11, 10 n. 15
Aquileian rite, 10–13, 16–18
Arcadelt, Jacques, 4–5, 30, 37, 72–3, 106–7; contrafactum in Treviso 29, 9
Ariosto, Ludovico, 39
Armstrong, James, 20–1, 23 n. 19
Arnold, Denis, 7 n. 7, 45, 53 n. 11
Arnoldo (Caussin?), 5, 98–9
Ascendit Deus in jubilatione (Clemens non Papa), 9 n. 14
Ascension, 22 n. 10, 32
Assumpsit Jesus Petrum et Jacobum et Joannem (Comes), 34, 80–1
Assumpta est Maria (Contino), 9, 35, 83
Assumption of the B.V.M., 10, 17, 97, 99
Atlas, Allan, 41 n. 24
Attaingnant, Pierre, 68–9
Auda, Antoine, 39 n. 20

Auribus percipe Domine (Phinot), 9, 35, 51, 75
Austriae stirpis (Contino), 9, 35, 83
Ave Confessor gloriose Liberalis (Verdelot), 9, 76–7
Ave et gaude gloriosa Virgo Maria (Willaert or Simon Ferrariensis), 100–1
Ave ignea columna (Cambio), 6, 9, 14, 86–7
Ave Maria alta stirps (Maitre Jhan or Jachet), 6, 8, 100–1
Ave Maria ancilla (Willaert), 100–1
Ave Maria gratia plena (antiphon), 51
Ave Maria gratia plena (cantus firmus), 111
Ave Maria gratia plena (Danckerts), 40 n. 21
Ave maris stella (Danckerts), 39 n. 20
Ave martir egregie o salutaris medice (Comes), 34, 74–5
Ave quam colunt angeli (Jachet), 34, 96–7
Ave Regina coelorum (antiphon), 25
Ave Regina coelorum (Zarlino), 35, 100–1
Ave sanctissima Maria Mater Dei (Anon.), 8, 100–1
Ave verum, 22
Ave Virgo gratiosa (Jachet), 34, 100–1
Ave Virgo sponsa Dei (Willaert), 34, 98–9
Ave vivens hostia (Contino), 9, 35, 89

Barre, Antonio, 40 n. 21
Basiron, Philippe, 54 n. 14
Bauldeweyn, Noel, 37, 112–13
Beata viscera Mariae Virginis (Willaert), 34, 96–7
Beati evangeliste Mathei (Contino), 9, 82–3
Beatissimus Marcus discipulus (Zarlino), 35–6, 76–7
Beatus Bernardus (Willaert), 7, 9, 14, 80–1
Beatus Dei famulus (Palestrina), 6, 8–9, 84–5
Beatus Laurentius orabat dicens (Willaert), 34, 80–1
Beausseron, Johannes, 30
Beheading of St John the Baptist, 14, 17, 83
Benedicamus Domino, 25 n. 30, 26 n. 32
Benedicta es coelorum Regina (Josquin), 30, 112–13
Benedicta es coelorum Regina (Willaert), 35, 44, 102–3
Benedicta et venerabilis (Portinaro), 37, 100–1, 110–11
Benedictus qui venit (Contino), 5, 9, 15 n. 29, 88–9
Benedictus Redemptor omnium (Willaert), 36, 80–1
Berchem, Jachet, 5, 36, 76–7, 96–7, 102–3
Bermudo, Juan, 40 n. 20

Bisan, Zanin, 32
Blackburn, Bonnie J., 7 n. 7, 70
Blume, C., 69
Bologna, 1
Bonifacio, Bartolomeo, 18 n. b, 25, 31, 69
Bragard, Anne-Marie, 71
Brescia, 13, 14 n. 26
Bridges, Thomas W., 7 n. 7
Brumel, Antoine, 30
Brumen, 30
Brunswick, Heinrich of, 37–8, 109
Bryant, David, 25 n. 28, 26 n. 33

Caeciliam cantate (Gombert), 9, 14, 35, 50, 93
Caeremoniale Episcoporum, 20, 27
Call, Jerry, 2 n. 1, 10 n. 15
Cambio, Perissone, 6, 86–7; contrafactum in Treviso 29, 9
Campagner, Mgr Angelo, vi, 52 n. 5
Canite tuba in Sion (Palestrina), 9, 14, 34, 93
Cantantibus organis (Rore), 9, 35, 89
Cantate caeli Domino (Anon.), 110–11
Cappella Giulia, 21 n. 10
Cappella Sistina, 39, 40 n. 21, 41; choir-books, 29–31; duties of singers, 22–3, 29; performance of motets in, 21–4, 26, 30–1, 36 n. 6; scriptorium, 45
Capponi, Neri, 38 n. 13
Casale Monferrato, 1
Casimiri, Raffaele, 37 n. 8, 44, 70
Caussin, Ernoul, 99. *See also* Arnoldo
Cavalli, Francesco, 21
Celle, 38
Cerone, Pedro, 39, 40 nn. 20–1
Chains of St Peter, 12, 17
Chair of St Peter at Antioch, 16, 75, 89
Chair of St Peter at Rome, 13, 16, 89
Chevalier, Ulysse, 69
Choirbooks, arrangement of, 29–31
Christi corpus ave (Scaffen), 106–7
Christi martir Sancte Chiliane (Willaert). *See* O Christi martir
Christmas. *See* Nativity of Our Lord
Circuire possum Domine (Angelo Palestrina), 34, 76–7
Circumcision of Our Lord, 16, 89
Cisilino, Siro, 43 nn. 30–1
Clangat plebs flores (Regis), 30
Clarus es ante alios (Danckerts), 40 n. 21
Claudin de Sermisy, 30
Clemens non Papa, 9 n. 14
Clement VIII, 20
Clementissime Deus (Maitre Jhan), 8, 37, 82–3, 108–9
Climent, José, 28 n. 39
Clodia quem genuit (Zarlino), 9, 35, 91
Columna es immobilis (Palestrina), 34, 86–7
Comes, Bartolomeo (Gallicus), 5, 34, 50, 67, 74–5, 80–3, 92–5, 98–9; contrafacta in Treviso 29, 9
Commemoration of St Paul, 12, 17
Common of Apostles, 10, 91

Common of Apostles and Evangelists, 10, 91
Common of Apostles in Paschaltide, 10, 91
Common of Apostles and Martyrs in Paschaltide, 10, 93
Common of a Confessor Bishop, 10, 93
Common of a Confessor not a Bishop, 10, 93, 95
Common of the Dedication of a Church, 10, 12, 95
Common of Doctors, 10, 93
Common of Holy Women, 10, 95
Common of Martyrs, 10, 93
Common of One Martyr, 10, 91
Common of Two or More Martyrs, 10, 93
Common of Two or More Virgin Martyrs, 10, 95
Common of Virgins, 10, 95
Common of Virgins and Holy Women, 10, 95
Communion, motets sung during, 21
Compère, Loyset, 36 n. 6
Conceptio tua Dei Genitrix (Gombert), 35, 104–5
Conception of the B.V.M., 10, 18, 97, 105
Confitemini Domino (Lasso), 9, 14, 35, 91
confraternities, music in, 23–4, 32–3
Confraternity of Corpus Christi, Treviso, 32
Confraternity of Our Lady, Antwerp, 23 n. 20
Confraternity of St Liberalis, Treviso, 32
Congrega, Domine (Palestrina), 9, 34, 97
Congregati sunt inimici (Werrecorre), 112–13
Contarini, Giovanni Battista, 37, 109
Contino, Giovanni, 5, 8, 14, 14 n. 26, 35, 37, 67, 78–93, 104–5, 110–11; contrafacta in Treviso 29, 9
contrafacta, 9, 13–15, 21, 36–9, 46–52, 55, 73–97
Conversion of St Paul, 16, 73, 89
Corona aurea (Palestrina), 34, 90–1
Corpus Christi, 32
Cortese, Paolo, 29
Corvo, Giovanni Battista, 5, 67, 74–7, 100–1
Council of Trent, 2, 10, 21 n. 10; discussion of music at, 28–9
counterpoint, 23, 28
Coussemaker, E. de, 1
Creator omnium Deus (Willaert), 9, 14, 34, 36, 93
Crecquillon, Thomas, 9 n. 14, 37, 73, 107
Crucem sanctam subiit (Danckerts), 40 n. 20
Cuglias, 37, 108–9
Culley, Thomas D., 22 n. 14
Cum iucunditate nativitatem (Comes), 9, 34, 50, 83, 98–9
Cum natus esset Jesus (Morales), 72–3, 106–7
Cummings, Anthony M., 21–2, 36 n. 6

Da ecclesiae tuae (Maitre Jhan), 6, 8, 36, 78–9
Da pacem (*cantus firmus*), 40–2, 113
Da pacem Domine (Portinaro), 9, 14, 35, 51, 93
D'Alessi, Giovanni, vi, 2, 4, 7–8, 9 nn. 12 and 14, 10 n. 15, 12 n. 22, 13 n. 25, 15, 31 nn. 45–8, 32, 33 n. 56, 34, 36 n. 7, 37–8, 41, 44–5, 52, 53 nn. 9–11, 54–5, 72, 79, 87, 93, 95, 106–7, 109, 113
Danckerts, Ghiselin, 5, 7 n. 7, 37, 39–44, 46–52, 56–8, 60–4, 72–3, 75, 110–11, 113; lost works, 40 n. 21; motet for Paul III, 40–43; *Suscipe Verbum*, 51–2, 60–4 (plates), 114–23 (transcription); treatise, 40 n. 21; *Tu es vas electionis*, 46–51, 56–8 (plates)
de Bruijn, J., vi, 39 n. 20, 43–4, 46
Dedication of the Basilica of the Saviour, 12, 18
Dedication of the Basilicas of SS Peter and Paul, 12, 18
Dedication of the Church of St Mark, 12, 17
Dedication of St Michael, 12, 17
Deo dicamus gratias (Festa), 26 n. 32
Deo gratias, motets sung in place of, 25, 26 n. 32; polyphonic settings, 26 n. 32
Deo gratias (H. Finck), 26 n. 32
Deo gratias (Ockeghem?), 26 n. 32
Deo gratias (Olivetto), 26 n. 32
Deo gratias (Tinctoris), 26 n. 32
Deo gratias (Philippe de Wildre), 26 n. 32
Descendi in hortum (Jachet), 96–7
Descendit Spiritus Sanctus (Phinot), 5, 9, 51, 72–3
Deus alma spes (Spalenza), 6, 9, 13, 36, 52–3, 84–5, 124–28 (transcription)
Deus cuius dextera (Contino), 5, 9, 80–1
Deus in nomine tuo (Ruffo), 112–13
Deus qui beatum (Contino), 5, 9, 88–9
Deus qui nobis sub sacramento (Contino), 9, 35–6, 81
Deus qui nos (Contino), 9, 82–3
Diem festum sacratissime (Arcadelt), 5, 9, 14, 15 n. 29, 37, 72–3
Dirigere et sanctificare (Santacroce), 106–7
Domine ante te (Testore), 9, 37, 77, 108–9
Domine Deus omnipotens (Santacroce), 52–3, 106–7, 129–34 (transcription)
Domine Jesu Christe fili Dei (Willaert), 9, 81
Domine ne in furore (Portinaro), 110–11
Domine ne longe facias (Comes), 9, 34, 75
Domine quis habitabit (Rore), 9, 15, 35, 81
Domus mea domus orationis (Comes), 34, 94–5
Doni, Antonfrancesco, 38 n. 13
Dorico, Valerio, 67
Dreves, G. M., 69
Dum esset summus pontifex (Portinaro), 6, 9, 14, 51, 92–3
Dum sacrum misterium (Garugli), 76–7

Easter, 32

Ecce tu pulchra es amica mea (Zarlino), 15 n. 28, 35, 98–9
Egregie Dei martir (antiphon), 14
Egregie martir Sebastiane (Gombert), 14, 72–3
Eisenhofer, Ludwig, 13 n. 24
Eitner, Robert, 38
Elegit te Dominus (Lasso), 6, 9, 88–9
Elevation, motets sung during, 21–2, 22 n. 12
11,000 virgins, 17, 83
Enceladi ceique soror (Jachet), 9, 34, 89
Enixa est puerpera (Willaert), 110–11
Epiphany, 8 n. 9, 10, 16, 73, 89, 107
Eripe me Domine (Portinaro), 108–9
Este, Alfonso d', 38
Exaltation of the Holy Cross, 12, 17
Exaudiat me Dominus (Rore), 9, 14, 35, 95

Fallows, David, 54 n. 16
falsobordone, 22–3, 52, 53 n. 9
Faulte d'argent (Danckerts), 40 n. 21
Feininger, Laurence, 43 n. 31
Felice sei Trevigi (Rore), 39
Felix nanque es (Anon.), 8, 100–1
Fellerer, K. G., 28 n. 39
Fenlon, Iain, 37 n. 8
Ferrara, 39
Ferrara, Cardinal of, 37 n. 8
Festa, Costanzo, 26 n. 32, 30, 36 n. 6
Févin, Antoine, 30
Fidel qual sempre fui (Danckerts), 40 n. 21
Filiae Jerusalem venite et videte (Palestrina), 6, 9, 14, 92–3
Finck, Heinrich, 26 n. 32
Finding of the Holy Cross, 16, 77
Finot. *See* Phinot
Florence, 22 n. 14
Forney, Kristine, 35 n. 4
Forty Holy Martyrs, 12, 16
Fremin, 30
Fuit homo missus (Palestrina), 34, 94–5
Fuit homo missus a Deo (Animuccia), 78–9

Gabriel angelus (Menchini), 106–7
Gabriel nunciavit Mariae (Phinot or Gombert), 5, 8, 74–5
Gallicus. *See* Comes
Gardane (Gardano), Antonio, 8, 34–6, 38–9, 44, 46, 50, 53, 67–9
Garilli. *See* Garugli
Garugli, Bernardino, 5, 67, 76–9, 90–1
Gascongne, Mathieu, 30
Gaspari, Gaetano, 53 n. 8
Gaude Barbara (Palestrina), 9, 34, 85
Gaude et laetare (Berchem), 5, 9, 36, 102–3
Gaude et laetare (Contino), 9, 84–5
Gaude Maria Virgo cunctas haereses (Rore), 35, 96–7
Gaudeamus [Willaert], 9, 82–3
Gaudeamus omnes (Willaert), 7, 9, 82–3
Gaudent in coelis anime sanctorum (Comes), 34, 92–3
Gaudent in coelis anime sanctorum (Garugli), 78–9

Gerstenberg, Walter, 71
Ghiselin, Johannes, 54 n. 14
Giamberti, Giuseppe, 20 n. 3
Giovanni di Liegi, 31
Gislinus. *See* Danckerts
Giuston, 37, 106–7
Glixon, Jonathan, 24
Gloriosum diem (Tugdual), 6, 15, n. 29, 36, 76–7
Gombert, Nicolas, 5, 7, 7 n. 7, 8, 14, 35–6, 50, 67–9, 72–5, 78–81, 86–7, 90–5, 104–5; contrafacta in Treviso 29, 9
Gonzaga, Guglielmo, 37 n. 8
Grandi, Alessandro, 21
Grandisson, Bishop John, 26 n. 32
Grassis, Paride de, 22
Gratias agimus (Danckerts), 40 n. 21

Haberl, Fr. X., 23 n. 16, 30 n. 43, 69
Haec est vera fraternitas (Palestrina), 6, 9, 14, 92–3
Hamm, Charles, 1 nn. 1–2, 4 n. 1, 10 n. 15, 31 n. 46
Harrison, Frank Ll., 26 n. 32
Hartwieg, Gisela, 40 n. 20
Hayburn, Robert S., 28 nn. 39–40
Hesdin, 30
Hic est dies egregius (Alberti), 5, 9, 36, 76–7
Hic est praecursor dilectus (Contino), 15 n. 29, 35, 78–9
Hic vir despiciens (Rore), 6, 9, 14, 94–5
Hodie beata Virgo Maria puerum (Contino), 35, 104–5
Hodie beata Virgo Maria puerum (Corvo), 74–5
Hodie Christus natus est (Contino), 35, 86–7
Hodie sanctus Benedictus (Zarlino), 7, 9, 14, 90–1
Hodie scietis (Rore), 6, 9, 86–7
Höfler, Janez, 70
Holy Innocents, 12, 16, 87

Il est bien aise (Danckerts), 40 n. 21
Illuminare Jerusalem (Phinot). *See* Surge illuminare Jerusalem
Illustra faciem tuam (Lasso), 9, 35, 89
Immensis beneficiis Hieronymum (Metallo), 108–9
In Domino confido (Rore), 9, 35, 50, 89
In ferventis olei (Testore), 6, 9, 14, 37, 76–7
In illo tempore dixit Jesus (Berchem), 76–7
In medio ecclesiae (Palestrina), 6, 9, 86–7
In te Domine speravi (Verdelot), 9, 77
In tua pacientia (Gombert), 5, 9, 15 n. 28, 86–7
Inclitae sanctae virginis (Palestrina), 34, 94–5
Infelix ego (Willaert), 110–11
Ingressus est Raphael (Giuston), 106–7
Innocentes pro Christo (Contino), 35, 86–7
Intervenientibus Domine (Contino), 5, 9, 80–1
Inviolata integra et casta es (sequence), 54
Inviolata integra et casta es (Anon.), 54 n. 14

Inviolata integra et casta es (Basiron), 54 n. 14
Inviolata integra et casta es (Ghiselin), 54 n. 14
Inviolata integra et casta es (Nasco), 6, 9, 36, 52, 54, 96–7, 135–42 (transcription)
Inviolata integra et casta es (Willaert), 35, 44, 102–3
Isaac, Heinrich, 41 n. 24
Iste est qui ante Deum (Contino), 5, 14, 92–3
Iste Sanctus pro lege Dei (Contino), 5, 9, 14, 90–1
Isti sunt viri sancti (Lupi), 9, 75
Istorum est enim regnum (Phinot), 35, 92–3
Ite, missa est, 21, 25 n. 30, 26, 26 n. 32
Jachet of Mantua, 5–6, 8, 14, 30, 36–7, 66, 68–9, 72–5, 84–5, 88–9, 91–3, 96–101, 106–7, 112–13; contrafacta in Treviso 29, 9
Jacobs, Charles, vi
Jam non dicam vos servos (Lupus or Richafort), 108–9
Janequin, Clément, 25
Jhan, Maitre, 5–6, 8, 30, 36–7, 41 n. 22, 78–85, 100–1, 108–13
John XXII, *Docta sanctorum*, 27
Johnson, Alvin H., 7 n. 7
Josquin des Prez, 1, 30, 36, 36 n. 6, 37, 70, 112–13
Jungmann, Joseph A., 22 n. 12
Juravit Dominus et non paenitebit (Gombert), 5, 9, 14, 50, 92–3

Kabis, Sister Mary Elise, 69, 109
Kriesstein, Melchior, 42

La Bataille de Marignan (Janequin), 25 n. 31
La dolce vista (Danckerts), 40 n. 21
La Fage, Adrien de, 41–2, 42 nn. 27–8
Laetamini in Domino (Danckerts), 39, 46
Laetare sancta mater ecclesia (Willaert), 106–7
Laetentur caeli (Contino), 9, 35, 89
Lafage, Johannes, 5–6, 78–9; contrafactum in Treviso 29, 9
Lasso, Orlando di, 4, 6–7, 14, 35, 68–9, 88–91; contrafacta in Treviso 29, 9
laude, 23–4
Laudemus Deum (Portinaro), 6, 9, 88–9
Laudemus Dominum (mistaken attribution to Rore), 6–8
Laudemus Dominum (Contino), 8–9, 90–1
Le Roy & Ballard, 68
Lechner, Joseph, 13 n. 24
Lenaerts, René, 27 n. 34
Leo X, 30
Lewis, Mary S., 35 n. 4, 36, 39 n. 16, 44 nn. 35–6
Lhéritier, Johannes, 30
Liberali, Giuseppe, 4 n. 2, 32 n. 51
Libertà, Giovan Francesco, 39
Llorens, José M., 20 n. 3, 30 n. 44, 41 n. 23
Lobo, Alonso, 30 n. 44
Lockwood, Lewis, 7 n. 7, 39, 53 n. 8

Loreto, 45
Louis XII, 1, 22 n. 12
Lowinsky, Edward E., vi, 5 n. 4, 9 n. 14,
  22 n. 12, 23 n. 20, 26 n. 32, 43 nn. 29–30
Luisetto, Giovanni, 43 n. 30
Lupi, Johannes, 6, 7 n. 7, 30, 68, 70, 74–5;
  contrafacta in Treviso 29, 9
Lupus, 4, 37, 108–9
Lusitano, Vicente, 39

Macey, Patrick, 70, 111
Magnificemus Deum salvatorum (Nasco),
  36, 88–9
Magnum misterium (Santacroce), 37, 72–3,
  106–7
Main, Alexander, 26 n. 32
Mantua, 37
Manuscripts, lost, 1–4
Manuscripts, musical
  Berlin 40021, 26 n. 32
  Bologna Q 12, 53
  Bologna Q 19, 65, 107
  Bologna Q 27, 101
  Bologna SP 31, 65, 79
  Bologna SP 39, 65, 107
  Brussels 27731, 39
  Cappella Giulia XV 29, 26 n. 32
  Copenhagen 1848, 26 n. 32
  C.S. 13, 30, 65, 107
  C.S. 15, 30
  C.S. 16, 30
  C.S. 17, 30
  C.S. 18, 26 n. 32, 30
  C.S. 19, 30
  C.S. 26, 30
  C.S. 29, 30
  C.S. 35, 30
  C.S. 38, 65, 79
  C.S. 44, 26 n. 32, 30
  C.S. 45, 30
  C.S. 46, 65, 111
  C.S. 55, 30
  C.S. 57, 30
  C.S. 63, 30
  C.S. 65, 26 n. 32
  C.S. 272, 26 n. 32
  Edinburgh 64, 65, 111
  Florence Palat. 6, 43 n. 30
  Florence 11, 65, 75
  Lucca 775, 36, 65, 79, 83
  Medici Codex, 95
  Modena C 313, 39, 44 n. 36, 65, 91, 107
  Modena C 314, 36, 39, 44 n. 36, 65, 79,
    109, 111
  Munich 45, 65, 113
  Munich B, 38, 65, 107
  Piacenza, 65, 101
  Regensburg AR 893, 66, 109, 111
  Strasbourg 222 C. 22, 1
  Toledo 17, 66, 75
  Treviso 3, 26 n. 32, 29, 43 n. 31
  Treviso 4, 10 n. 15, 36, 53 n. 11, 83, 85,
    107, 113
  Treviso 5, 10 n. 15, 36, 77, 83
  Treviso 6, 10 n. 15, 36, 79
  Treviso 7, 8 n. 15, 10, 36, 45 n. 37, 53, 79
  Treviso 8, 10 n. 15, 36, 45 n. 37, 75, 89
  Treviso 10, 26 n. 32, 45 n. 37
  Treviso 11, 45 n. 37, 53
  Treviso 12, 29
  Treviso 13, 36, 45 n. 37, 53
  Treviso 14, 45 n. 37
  Treviso 18, 29
  Treviso 22, 53
  Treviso 24, 45 n. 37, 53
  Treviso 25, 26 n. 32, 29
  Treviso 29: concordances in other
    Trevisan MSS, 36; contrafacta in, 9,
    13–15, 46–51, 73–97; date, 14, 34;
    inventory, 72–105; liturgical cycle,
    10–18; owner, 4; physical descrip-
    tion, 44–5; relation of texts to liturgy,
    15; sources, 34–6; texts, 15; unica,
    4–10, 36
  Treviso 30, 4, 7, 10 n. 15, 51, 53–4, 73,
    77, 83; date, 45; inventory, 106–13;
    physical description, 44–5; repertory,
    37–43; unica, 38–9, 52
  Treviso 36, 10 n. 15, 81, 85, 107
  Uppsala 76c, 54 n. 14
  Vallicelliana, 66, 91
  Wolfenbüttel 293, 36, 39, 66, 79, 83, 111
Manuscripts, other
  Vallicelliana R 56, 40 n. 21
  Venice Cod. Lat. III-172 [=2276], 18 n.
    b, 25 nn. 28 and 31, 69
  Venice Codice Cicogna 1602, 18 n. b
  Venice Scuole piccole B. 396bis, 33 n. 56
Maria stabat ad monumentum (Contino), 9,
  35, 87
Matthias. See Werrecorre
Medici, Cosimo de', 43
Medici stemma, 41, 43
Meier, Bernhard, 7–8, 39 nn. 17–18, 70
Meissner, Ute, 35 n. 4
Memor esto verbi tui (Josquin), 30
Memor esto verbi tui (Nasco), 52, 54–5,
  110–11, 142–44 (transcription)
Menchini, Benedetto, 106–7
Merlo, Giovanni Antonio, 36 n. 6
Merritt, A. Tillman, 69
Metallo, Grammatio, 37, 45, 108–9
Milan, 1
Miseremini mei (Contino), 110–11
Miserere nostri Deus (Willaert), 9, 35, 44,
  79, 83
Misit rex incredulus (Comes), 9, 14, 15 n.
  28, 50, 82–3
Missa Benedicta es coelorum regina, 30
Missa de Beata Virgine, 30
Missa della bataglia (Janequin?), 25, 28 n.
  39
Missa Ducalis (Porta), 43
Missa Surge Petre (Jachet), 112–13
Missa Surge Petre (Portinaro), 112–13
Mittit ad virginem (Willaert), 35
Moderne, Jacques, 14
Monteverdi, Claudio, 20, 25 n. 31

Moore, James H., vi, 10 n. 15, 11, 18 n. b, 21, 24–5, 27
Morales, Cristóbal de, 4, 8, 30, 37–8, 70, 72–3, 75, 106–9
Moreau, Simon, 8, 75
motets: function of, 19–33; liturgical cycles, 19–21
Mouton, Jean, 30, 36, 36 n. 6
Mulier quae erat (Rore), 6, 9, 14–15, 80–1
Murus tuus dilecta (Jachet), 98–9

Naples, 41
Nasco, Giovanni, 5–6, 13, 31, 36–7, 43 n. 31, 45, 52, 54–5, 88–9, 96–7, 110–11; *Inviolata, integra et casta es*, 54, 135–42 (transcription); *Memor esto*, 54–5, 142–4 (transcription)
Nativity of the B.V.M., 10, 17, 99
Nativity of St John the Baptist, 17, 79, 95
Nativity of Our Lord, 10, 16, 23, 73, 87, 101, 105
Nausea, Federicus, Bishop of Vienna, 28–9
Ne derelinquas me Domine (Cuglias), 108–9
Neri, San Filippo, 23–4
Newcomb, Anthony, 38 n. 14
Non est in hominis potestate (Alberti), 108–9
Non m'è grave el tormento (Danckerts), 40 n. 21
Non vos me elegistis (Lasso), 35, 90–1
Nos autem gloriari oportet (Corvo), 15 n. 29, 76–7
Nugent, George, 7 n. 7, 8 n. 8, 69, 73

O admirabile commercium (Contino), 9, 35, 81
O beatum pontificem (Willaert), 34, 36, 84–5
O beatum pontificem (Zarlino), 9, 14, 35, 93
O beatum virum (Contino), 35, 84–5
O Christi martir sancte Chiliane (Willaert), 6, 9, 80–1
O doctor optime (Willaert), 7, 9, 14, 92–3
O felix Anna (Gombert), 35, 80–1
O felix custos (Jachet), 6, 9, 14, 74–5
O felix custos martirum (Maitre Jhan), 110–11
O gloriosa Domina (Willaert), 34, 96–7
O Gregori (Rore), 6, 88–9
O lampas ardens (Jachet), 72–3
O lux et decus Hispaniae (Palestrina), 34, 94–5
O lux Italiae (Lasso), 6, 9, 88–9
O magnum mysterium (Contino), 9, 35, 80–1
O martir egregie (Comes). See *Ave martir egregie*
O praesul venerabilis (Jachet), 6, 9, 84–5
O proles Hispaniae (Willaert), 36, 78–9
O quam gloriosum est regnum (Contino), 84–5
O quam gloriosum est regnum (Phinot), 35, 82–3
O quam magnificum (Contino), 5, 9, 80–1
O quam metuendus (Palestrina), 34, 94–5

O quam praeclara sunt (Jachet), 9, 75, 85
O sacrum convivium, 22
O salutaris hostia, 22
O sancte praesul Nicolae (Palestrina), 34, 84–5
O sodales sancti Vindemialis et Florentii (Willaert), 6, 9, 78–9
O stupor et gaudium (Contino), 9, 14, 35, 93
O Virgo simul et Mater, lux maxima mundi (Palestrina), 9, 34, 87, 100–1
Ockeghem, Johannes, 26 n. 32
Octave of Epiphany, 73, 107
Octave of Holy Innocents, 12, 16
Octave of SS Peter and Paul, 17, 81
Octave of St John, 12, 16
Octave of St Martin, 18
Octave of St Stephen, 12, 16
Octave of the Visitation, 13 n. 24, 17
Offertory, motets sung during, 21–2, 26–7, 28 n. 39, 36 n. 6
Olivetto, Nicolò, 26 n. 32, 32, 43 n. 31
Omnipotens sempiterne Deus (Contino), 9, 80–1
Omnipotens sempiterne Deus (Palestrina), 34, 96–7
oratorio vespertino, 23–4
Oratory of San Filippo Neri, 23–4
Osculetur me osculo oris sui (Phinot), 35, 98–9
Owens, Jessie Ann, 7 n. 7, 38 n. 15

Pace, Giovanni, 25 n. 31
Padua, 8 n. 11, 37
Palestrina, Angelo Pierluigi, 76–7
Palestrina, Giovanni Pierluigi da, 5–9, 14, 34, 42, 68, 70, 77–9, 84–7, 90–7, 100–1; contrafacta in Treviso 29, 9
Palisca, Claude V., 7 n. 7
Palle, palle (Isaac), 41 n. 24
Paolucci, Giuseppe, 70, 99
Papal Chapel. See Cappella Sistina
Parma, 39
Partus et integritas (Lafage), 9, 36, 79
Patavino. See Santacroce
Patefactae sunt ianuae (Contino), 5, 9, 86–7
Pater noster (Danckerts), 40 n. 21
Pater noster (Rore), 38, 106–7
Paul III, 28, 30, 40–1, 113
Paul IV, 13
Peccantem me quotidie (Palestrina), 9, 34, 87
Peccata mea (Willaert), 108–9
Pecorina, Polisena, 38
Penet, Hilaire, 30
Pentecost, 32
Perche piangi Alma (Danckerts), 40 n. 21
Perissonus. See Cambio
Petite camusette (Danckerts), 40 n. 21
Petre amas me (Rore), 6, 9, 50, 88–9
Phinot, Dominicus, 5, 8, 35–6, 46–51, 68, 70, 72–7, 82–5, 92–3, 98–9; contrafacta in Treviso 29, 9
Pierreson. See Cambio
Pieton, Loyset, 30
Pinsonio, Jacobo, 37 n. 8

Pionnier, Johannes, 36
Pipelare, Matthaeus, 30, 36 n. 6
Pirrotta, Nino, 29 n. 42
Più volte già dal bel sembiante (Willaert), 9, 35, 44, 81
Pius V, breviary of 1568, 10–11, 13, 21 n. 10
Pius X, Motu Proprio on Sacred Music, 27 n. 37
Porta, Costanzo, 36, 43
Portinaro, Francesco, 5–6, 14, 35, 37, 51, 68, 88–9, 92–3, 96–101, 104–5, 108–13; contrafacta in Treviso 29, 9
Praecamur te Pater (Santacroce), 53 n. 11
Praeceptor bonum est (Palestrina), 6, 9, 96–7
Praesul sanctissime Augustine (Maitre Jhan), 8, 36, 82–3
Praeter rerum ordinem (Willaert), 35, 44, 104–5
Praeter rerum seriem (Josquin), 30
Presentation of the B.V.M., 13 n. 24, 18
Prints:
 Animuccia 1552, 67, 79
 Antico 1521[5], 66, 79
 Barre 1555[27], 39, 40 n. 21
 Comes 1547, 34, 67, 75, 81, 83, 93, 95, 99
 Continus 1560/1, 35, 67, 79, 81, 83, 85, 87, 89, 93
 Continus 1560/2, 35, 67, 83, 87, 91, 93, 105
 Continus 1560/3, 67, 85
 Corvus 1555, 67, 75, 77, 101
 Gardane 1539[3], 66, 97
 Gardane 1542[10], 34, 66, 81, 85, 97, 99, 101
 Gardane 1544[6], 66, 81
 Gardane 1549[6], 8, 34, 66, 73, 91, 95, 97, 99, 101
 Gardane 1549[8], 34, 66, 87, 89, 93, 95, 97, 99
 Gardane 1553[17], 66, 73, 75, 77, 85, 99
 Garulli 1562, 67, 77, 79, 91
 Gombert 1541, 67, 79, 81, 91, 93, 105
 Gombert 1550, 35, 68, 79, 81, 91, 105
 Gombert 1552, 35, 68, 87, 95
 Jachet 1540, 68, 101
 Jachet 1557, 68, 113
 Kriesstein 1540[7], 40, 42, 66, 111, 113
 Kriesstein 1545[3], 66, 73, 75, 113
 Lasso 1562, 35, 68, 89, 91
 Lupi 1542, 68, 75
 Moderne 1532[9], 66, 73, 75, 99, 101
 Moderne 1538[2], 66, 75, 77
 Moderne 1542[5], 66, 93, 99
 Montanus & Neuber 1554[10], 66, 107
 Montanus & Neuber 1555[11], 66, 73
 Montanus & Neuber [1556][9], 67, 111
 Palestrina 1572, 34, 68, 77, 79, 85, 87, 91, 93, 101
 Palestrina 1575, 34, 68, 85, 87, 91, 93, 95, 97
 Petreius 1542[6], 26 n. 32
 Petrucci, Motetti L. IV, 54 n. 14

Phalèse 1553[11], 67, 75
Phinot 1547, 35 n. 3, 50
Phinot 1552, 35, 46, 50, 68, 73, 75, 77, 83, 85, 93, 99
Portinaro 1548, 35, 68, 89, 93, 97, 99, 105
Portinaro 1568, 37, 68, 101, 109, 111
Rhau 1545[5], 67, 107
Rore 1545, 35, 39, 68, 81, 87, 89, 95, 97, 99
Rore 1595, 91
Ruffo 1555, 68, 113
Schoeffer 1539[8], 67, 101, 107
Scotto 1541[3], 67, 75, 107
Susato 1546[7], 67, 75
Susato 1557[3], 67, 75
Ulhard 1545[2], 26 n. 32, 39, 46
Willaert 1539 or 1550, 68, 81, 101, 107
Willaert 1559 (*Musica nova*), 35, 38, 44–5, 59 (plate), 69, 79, 81, 83, 103, 105, 109
Zarlino 1549, 35, 69, 77, 91, 93, 99, 101
Zarlino 1566, 69, 89, 99
Prudens et vigilans (Contino), 35, 84–5
Prudentes virgines aptate lampades (Rore), 6, 9, 14, 94–5
Pruett, Lilian P., 43 n. 30
Pulchrior italicis (Rore), 9, 35, 87
Purification of the B.V.M., 10, 16, 73, 75, 105

Qualis es dilecta mea (Berchem), 96–7
Quando fra l'altre donne (Willaert), 9, 35, 44, 83
Qui vult venire (Lasso), 6, 9, 14, 90–1
Quia vidisti me Thoma (Contino), 5, 9, 86–7
Quis tuus has nostras (Portinaro), 38, 108–9

Rampazetto, F., 69
Regina coeli (Portinaro), 35, 104–5
Regis, Johannes, 30
Regnum mundi (responsory), 51
Regnum mundi (Rore), 6, 9, 14, 51, 94–5
Repleatur os meum (Jachet), 9, 14, 93
Richafort, Johannes, 5, 30, 37, 94–5, 109
Roman rite, 10–13, 13 n. 24, 14, 16–18
Rome, 23–4
Rore, Cipriano de, 1, 5–7, 7 n. 7, 8, 14–15, 35, 37–8, 38 n. 12, 39, 50–1, 66, 68, 70, 80–1, 86–9, 91, 94–9, 106–9; contrafacta in Treviso 29, 9
Rosa de spinis protulit (Arnoldo), 98–9
Rosand, Ellen, 11 n. 19
Rovetta, Giovanni, 21
Ruer, 113
Ruffo, Vincenzo, 37, 68, 112–13
Ruhnke, Martin, 38 n. 9

Sacerdos et pontifex (Contino), 5, 9, 14, 92–3
Sacrae legis Christianae (Maitre Jhan), 6, 8, 36, 82–3
Salve sancta parens (Willaert), 35, 44, 102–3
Sancta et immaculata (Palestrina), 34, 100–1
Sancta et immaculata (Portinaro), 9, 35, 89

Sancta Maria Virgo virginum (Crecquillon), 9 n. 14
Sancte Francisce propere (Willaert), 36, 82–3
Sancte Gregori (Gombert), 5, 74–5
Sancte Jacobe apostole (Maitre Jhan), 80–1
Sancte Marce (Anon.), 110–11
Sancte Marce evangelista (Lupi), 6, 9, 74–5
Sancte Paule apostole (Lafage), 6, 9, 14, 36, 78–9
Sancti Dei omnes (Contino), 15 n. 28, 35–6, 84–5
Sanctificavit Dominus tabernaculum (Palestrina), 34, 94–5
Sanctorum martyrum tuorum (Contino), 9, 14, 35, 93
Sandberger, A., 69
Sansovino, Francesco, 25 n. 28, 26 n. 33
Santacroce, Francesco (Patavino), 5, 7 n. 7, 31, 32 n. 49, 37, 45, 52–4, 72–3, 106–7; *Domine Deus omnipotens*, 52–54, 129–34 (transcription)
Savonarola, Girolamo, 111
Scaffen, Henricus, 5–6, 36–8, 72–3, 106–7
Scarpello si vedrà (Danckerts), 40 n. 21
Scattolin, Pier Paolo, 14
Schmidt-Görg, Joseph, 69
Schmieder, Wolfgang, 40 n. 20
Scotto, Girolamo, 34–5, 38, 67–8
scuole grandi, music in, 24, 27
Seay, Albert, 26 n. 32
Sebastianus Dei cultor (antiphon), 14
Sebastianus Dei cultor (Zarlino), 14, 88–9
Senex puerum portabat (Scaffen), 6, 9, 36, 72–3
Servus tuus ego sum (ostinato in Nasco's *Memor esto*), 55
Sforza family, 1
Sherr, Richard, 22 nn. 10, 15, 36 n. 6
Si ignoras te (Rore), 35, 98–9
Si resurrexistis una cum Christo (Rore), 38–9, 108–9
Sicut cedrus exaltata sum (Portinaro), 35, 98–9
Sicut lilium inter spinas (Anon.), 8, 96–7
Signum salutis (Arcadelt or Crecquillon), 9, 37, 73, 106–7
Silvester beatissimus (Palestrina), 6, 9, 14, 86–7
Similabo eum (Jachet), 6, 9, 14, 92–3
Simon Ferrariensis, 101
Sistine Chapel. *See* Cappella Sistina
Slim, H. Colin, vi
Smijers, A., 70, 113
Smither, Howard E., 24 n. 21
Spalenza, Pietro Antonio, 5–6, 13–14, 14 n. 26, 36, 52–3, 84–5; *Deus alma spes*, 52–3, 124–28 (transcription)
Sparks, Edgar H., 70, 113
St Agatha, 14, 16, 75
St Agnes, 14, 16, 73, 89
St Ambrose, 14, 18, 87
St Andrew, 18, 85
St Anne, 13 n. 24, 17, 81
St Anthony, Abbot, 16, 73, 89, 109

St Anthony of Padua, 13 n. 24, 17, 73, 79
St Apollonia, 16, 75
St Augustine, 17, 83, 107
St Bacchus, 18 n. j
St Barnabas, 12, 17
St Bartholomew, 17, 81, 97
St Benedict, 10, 14, 16, 91
St Bernard of Clairvaux, 14, 17, 81
St Blaise, 14–16, 75, 89
St Catherine, 18, 85, 95
St Cecilia, 18, 18 n. k
St Dominic, 17, 81
SS Fabian and Sebastian, 14, 16, 73, 89
SS Florentius and Vindemialis, 8, 8 n. 11, 17, 79
St Fortunatus, 8, 8 n. 11
St Francis, 17, 83
St Gregory, 16, 75, 89
SS Hermacoras and Fortunatus, 8, 8 n. 11, 13 n. 24, 17, 81
St James, 12 n. 23, 16–17, 77, 81, 95
St Jerome, 17, 83, 109
St Joachim, 13, 16, 91
St John, Apostle, 12, 16, 87
St John, Baptist, 14, 17, 79, 83, 95
St John before the Lateran Gate, 14, 17, 77
St Joseph, 14, 16, 75, 91
St Jude, 17, 83
St Justina, 17, 83
St Kylianus, 8 n. 11, 17, 81
St Lawrence, 17, 81
St Leonard, 13, 18 n. h.
St Liberalis, 8, 8 n. 11, 12 n. 23, 16, 32–3, 36, 77
St Longinus, 12, 13 n. 24, 16
St Lucy, 18, 87
St Luke, 17, 83
St Mark, 10 n. 15, 12, 13 n. 24, 16, 75, 77
St Mark, Pope, 17
St Mark's, Venice, 21; duties of singers, 24–7; liturgy, 8 n. 11, 10–13, 16–18, 31, 73; musical repertory, 1; performance of motets in, 24–7
St Martin, 18, 85
St Mary Magdalene, 14–15, 17, 81
St Matthew, 17, 83
St Matthias, 16, 89
St Maurus, 18
St Michael, 12, 17, 77
St Nicholas, 18, 85
St Patrick, 12, 13 n. 24, 16
St Paul, 12, 16–17, 73, 89
St Peter, 12–13, 16–17, 75, 89
SS Peter and Paul, 12, 17, 79, 81
St Peter's, Rome, 22 n. 10
SS Philip and James, 12, 16, 77
St Prisca, 12, 16
St Prosdocimus, 8, 8 n. 11, 13 n. 24, 15, 18, 85
St Raphael, 107
St Roch, 13, 13 n. 24, 17, 18 n. h, 81
SS Sergius and Bacchus, 18 n. j
St Silvester, 14, 16, 87

SS Simon and Jude, 17, 83
St Stephen, 12, 16, 87
St Theodore, 18
SS Theonistus, Tabra and Tabrata, 8–9, 8 n. 11, 13, 18, 53, 85
St Thomas, Apostle, 18, 87
St Thomas Aquinas, 16, 89
St Titianus, 12, 16
St Vindemialis, 8, 8 n. 11, 17, 79
SS Vitus, Modestus and Crescentia, 17, 79
Stäblein, Bruno, 70, 111
Stadiis, Clemens a, 11–12, 14, 31
Stans beata Agnes (Jachet), 6, 88–9
Strozzi, Ruberto, 38 n. 12
Sub tuum presidium (Willaert), 35, 44, 102–3
Sufficiebat nobis paupertas (Jachet), 106–7
Sugana, Liberale, 31, 45 n. 38
Surge illuminare Jerusalem (Phinot), 5, 8, 15 n. 29, 72–3
Surge Petre et indue te (Contino), 9, 35, 91
Surge Petre et indue te (Gombert), 35, 78–9
Surge Petre et indue te (Jachet), 91, 113
Surge propera amica mea speciosa mea (Corvo), 100–1
Surrexit pastor bonus (Lasso), 9, 35, 89
Susato, Tielman, 35 n. 4
Suscipe Verbum Virgo Maria (Anon.), 8, 15 n. 29, 100–1
Suscipe Verbum Virgo Maria (Danckerts), 39, 51–2, 60–4 (plates), 110–11, 114–23 (transcription)
Suscipe Verbum Virgo Maria (Gombert), 36, 74–5

Tagmann, Pierre, 37 n. 8
Tanto tempore vobiscum sum (Phinot), 9, 35, 51, 73, 76–7
Te gloriosus apostolorum (Comes), 34, 82–3
Te gloriosus apostolorum (Phinot), 35, 84–5
Tempus est ut revertar (Contino), 9, 35, 87
Testore, Guglielmo, 5–6, 37, 37 n. 8, 76–7, 108–9; contrafactum in Treviso 29, 9
Texebat viridem cloris (Contino), 9, 35, 81, 85
Tiepolo, Patriarch Giovanni, 27
Tinctoris, Johannes, 23, 26 n. 32
Torchi, Luigi, 70, 99
Tout d'ung accord (Danckerts), 40 n. 21
Tradent enim vos (Palestrina), 34, 90–1
Transfiguration of Our Lord, 17, 81, 97
Translation of St Mark, 12, 13 n. 24, 16
Treviso, 1
Treviso Cathedral: destruction of library, 2; liturgy, 8, 10–19, 31, 73 n. 1; lost manuscripts, 2–4, 7–8; musical repertory, 1–2, 10 n. 15, 12 n. 23, 29, 31, 45; Ordinal of 1524, 9 n. 13, 11–18, 31, 70, 73 n. 1; performance of motets in, 31–3
Tristis est anima mea (Nasco), 52
Tu Domine universorum (Bauldeweyn), 112–13
Tu es Petrus (Gombert, Morales or Moreau), 5, 8, 74–5

Tu es Petrus (Palestrina), 34, 78–9
Tu es vas electionis (Danckerts), 5, 43 n. 32, 46–51, 56–8 (plates), 72–3
Tua est potentia (Danckerts or Maitre Jhan), 40–2, 52, 112–13
Tua est potentia (Phinot), 9, 35, 46–51, 73
Tugdual, 5–6, 7 n. 7, 76–7

unica, 5–9, 36, 38, 52, 55
Usquequo Domine (Rore), 9, 14, 35, 51, 95
Ut te muneribus (Contino), 9, 14, 35, 91

Valencia Cathedral, performance of motets in, 28 n. 39
Van Dijk, S. J. P., 8 n. 11
Varisco, Pietro, 9–10, 14, 32–6, 45–6, 48–51, 55; owner of Treviso 29, 4
Veni dilecta mea (Gombert), 9, 35, 87
Veni electa mea (Gombert), 35, 94–5
Veni in hortum meum (Lasso), 9, 35, 89
Veni sponsa Christi (Anon.), 8, 94–5
Veni sponsa Christi (Richafort), 94–5
Venice, 1, 10 n. 15, 24, 39, 54
Venite ad me omnes qui laboratis (Gombert), 35, 90–1
Verdelot, Philippe, 71, 76–7; contrafactum in Treviso 29, 9
Veretoni, Francesco, 12 n. 23, 45
Vicentino, Nicola, 39, 42
Victory of St Michael, 17, 77
Videntes stellam Magi gavisi sunt (Lasso), 35, 88–9
Vidi speciosam sicut columbam (Lupi), 9, 75
Vidi speciosam sicut columbam (Portinaro), 15 n. 29, 35, 96–7
Vigil of Epiphany, 25 n. 29
Vigil of the Nativity of Our Lord, 18, 22 n. 10, 25 n. 29, 87
Virgo Maria speciosissima (Anon.), 8, 98–9
Virgo martir (Comes), 5, 9, 74–5
Virgo prudentissima (Zarlino), 98–9
Virgo salutiferi (Josquin), 30
Virtute magna reddebant (Rore?), 8, 90–1
Visitation of the B.V.M., 10, 13, 17, 99, 101
Vocatus Joseph (Garugli), 90–1

Weinmann, Karl, 28 n. 39
Werrecorre, Hermann Mathias, 37, 112–13
Wildre, Philippe de, 26 n. 32
Willaert, Adrian, 1, 5–7, 7 n. 7, 14, 30, 34–8, 44–5, 59, 66, 68–9, 71, 78–85, 92–3, 96–111; contrafacta in Treviso 29, 9
Willaert, Alvise, 36
Wolfenbüttel, 38 n. 9, 40 n. 20
Würzburg, 8 n. 11

Zarlino, Gioseffo, 1, 5, 7, 7 n. 7, 14, 35, 69, 76–7, 88–93, 98–101; contrafacta in Treviso 29, 9
Zenck, Hermann, 71
Ziino, Agostino, vi